Healing Ancestral Karma

Heal Your Ancestors and Family Tree of Karmic Debt, Unhealthy Patterns and Lingering Trauma

© Copyright 2025 - All rights reserved.

The content contained within this book may not be reproduced, duplicated, or transmitted without direct written permission from the author or the publisher.

Under no circumstances will any blame or legal responsibility be held against the publisher or author for any damages, reparation, or monetary loss due to the information contained within this book, either directly or indirectly.

Legal Notice:

This book is copyright-protected. It is only for personal use. You cannot amend, distribute, sell, use, quote, or paraphrase any part of the content within this book without the consent of the author or publisher.

Disclaimer Notice:

Please note the information contained within this document is for educational and entertainment purposes only. All effort has been executed to present accurate, up-to-date, reliable, and complete information. No warranties of any kind are declared or implied. Readers acknowledge that the author is not engaging in the rendering of legal, financial, medical, or professional advice. The content within this book has been derived from various sources. Please consult a licensed professional before attempting any techniques outlined in this book.

By reading this document, the reader agrees that under no circumstances is the author responsible for any losses, direct or indirect, that are incurred as a result of the use of the information contained within this document, including, but not limited to, errors, omissions, or inaccuracies.

Your Free Gift
(only available for a limited time)

Thanks for getting this book! If you want to learn more about various spirituality topics, then join Mari Silva's community and get a free guided meditation MP3 for awakening your third eye. This guided meditation mp3 is designed to open and strengthen ones third eye so you can experience a higher state of consciousness. Simply visit the link below the image to get started.

https://spiritualityspot.com/meditation

Or, Scan the QR code!

Table of Contents

INTRODUCTION 1
CHAPTER ONE: THE SPIRITUAL ROOTS AND SCIENCE OF ANCESTRAL KARMA 3
CHAPTER TWO: TRACING THE LINEAGE OF PAIN AND TRAUMA 16
CHAPTER THREE: UNCOVERING THE FAMILY SHADOW 29
CHAPTER FOUR: THE CALL TO HEALING: PREPARING FOR THE JOURNEY 45
CHAPTER FIVE: RELEASING RITUALS: THE PATH TO FORGIVENESS 60
CHAPTER SIX: BREAKING THE CHAINS: HEALING GENERATIONAL PATTERNS 74
CHAPTER SEVEN: HONORING THE ANCESTORS: REBUILDING BONDS AND RECLAIMING POWER 86
CHAPTER EIGHT: CREATING A NEW LEGACY: SPREADING HEALING ACROSS GENERATIONS 95
CONCLUSION 104
HERE'S ANOTHER BOOK BY MARI SILVA THAT YOU MIGHT LIKE 107
YOUR FREE GIFT (ONLY AVAILABLE FOR A LIMITED TIME) ... 108
REFERENCES 109
IMAGE SOURCES 110

Introduction

"The gods visit the sins of the father on the children."

This is a quote by Euripides, a famous Greek playwright who lived around 400 B.C. There are many versions of this provocative quote today, but its meaning has never changed: Everyone is affected, in part, by the lives and mistakes of those who came before them. It's a heavy truth this one, and it comes with great power and great responsibility.

The difference between the person searching for answers and those who haven't awakened to this reality yet is a heightened awareness. You're here because you want to understand the generational imprint carried over from your ancestors. The unawakened are blissfully unaware, and they move through the world, reactive and disempowered, without a clue why they feel the way they do or why particular patterns keep repeating in their lives. And you know what they say: you can't fix a problem you don't know exists in the first place.

This book is here to teach you to identify the beliefs and emotions that may have been handed down to you, usually silently and unconsciously. These inherited energies manifest as trends, fears, tendencies, or health issues, but they don't have to define you. It is possible to break free, and that begins with understanding what the problem is and where it came from. This book is written comprehensively and simplistically to make this complex topic easy to digest.

There will be exercises at the end of every chapter because practice is the best way to learn. Nothing about this is theoretical. You're not just here to read; you're also going to integrate the lessons into your life AS you read. This way, it sticks.

You are healing the past for the sake of the present and setting a better precedent for the future. You are one link in an unbroken chain stretching back thousands of years into the past and forward into an unknowable future. For all their flaws and shortcomings, your ancestors managed to survive and pass on the gift of life. Through wars, famines, plagues, oppression, and pain, they kept going. And now, here you are, the beneficiary of their tenacity. You're not just living for yourself but for all the souls in your bloodline who dreamed of a better future. The things you will learn in this book will hopefully allow you to leave the world a little bit brighter than you found it. You have a sacred mission to fulfill, and if you wonder if it's all worth it, it is.

Chapter One: The Spiritual Roots and Science of Ancestral Karma

Actions have consequences; that's karma's number one rule. What goes around comes around, and every single choice counts. You get what you give, maybe not in this lifetime, but your energy will find its way back to you. Karma is not retribution. People hear consequences and assume they have to be negative, but consequences can also be positive. Karma is neither positive nor negative; it just is. Karma is balance, it is divine justice, and it is a teaching mechanism.

Karma is something that is in your hands alone.[1]

There's a belief that your karma is yours and yours alone, but if only it were that simple. Karma's reach touches families, communities, and, sometimes, the entire human collective. Your karma is intertwined with that of every member of your bloodline, and the result is consequences that extend throughout generations. You can find whole families suffering from the same problem, from the head of the family to the very last child.

A family suffering from addictive tendencies, for instance, would assume it's only a coincidence, a personal struggle, or learned behavior. It may look like that on the surface, but when you pull on the threads of this weave, the whole thing unravels, and you see that this habit goes back to traumas or choices made by ancestors long ago. The pain, shame, and unprocessed emotions of these ancestors have become a spiritual inheritance, passed down to their descendants and the descendants after that, and so on. Karma then becomes a family artifact, except instead of being similar to a royal hairpin or an estate, it's a generational blight – an energetic weight that each new generation has to shoulder, whether they know it or not.

Another good example is poverty. If your grandparents struggled to put food on the table, your parents never quite managed to get ahead, leading you to be in a similar predicament. It's fair to conclude that this is just your luck in life, a curse you were born into, the cards you were dealt, but it's not. Not really. This is a financial pattern, and it keeps repeating because of the latent energies passed down your family tree. Your grandparents may have believed that money is scarce, that they'll never have enough. It's only a belief; it seems harmless, doesn't it? It isn't. What looked like an innocent assumption could've caused them to make decisions that led to the very outcomes they were afraid of. Children are bound to inherit the subconscious beliefs and emotional tendencies of their parents, so those same beliefs get passed on to the next generation – your parents.

This simple principle could be applied to any recurring problem in your family, such as addiction, toxic relationships, and chronic health problems. All of these patterns go back through your family tree, which means they can be healed to change not just your own life but the trajectory of your entire lineage.

Just to be clear, your family's karma does not solely define you. Your destiny is your own, and it is more than possible to rise above the limitations of your upbringing and create something brand new. But these karmic undercurrents don't just disappear, and they are better handled with awareness and intention so they don't weasel their way into your children's lives.

The Energetic Truth of the Family Tree

To the untrained eye, a family tree is made only of names and dates, but that's not all it's made of. If you know what to look for, you'll see that it's actually a pulsating map; it is your family's energetic legacy. You are part of a collective energy field. Another name for it is family. Your great-great-grandfather, your grandmother, and your cousins twice removed – they all contribute to this energy field. Yes, there are physical features or talents everyone shares – you could all have a cleft chin or the same striking eye color – but this energetic legacy is something else entirely. In your collective energy field, you also share psychological predispositions, spiritual habits, and intuitive gifts that have been selectively sharpened over generations.

There are many traits shared through your family tree.²

These traits are carried by energetic currents that flow through the entire family tree. And those currents? They don't just flow downward from the generation above to the one below. They also flow sideways, connecting siblings, cousins, and distant relatives in ways that may or may not be obvious. These currents can also reach back into the past, with a direct link that stretches between you and the lives of your ancestors from 300 years ago. You may be afraid of water, and your fear feels instinctive, even though you've never been traumatized by water. There's the possibility that it is a karmic pattern from a past life, OR it could be that your great-grandmother was shipwrecked at sea, and that memory, still very much alive in the family's collective energy field, manifested in you. It sounds unbelievable and possibly far-fetched, but science has actual proof of this, and it is called Epigenetics.

Epigenetics

Epigenetics is a scientific field that studies how environmental factors can turn genes on or off without actually changing the DNA sequence. It turns out there is a dimmer switch for every gene. The same genes are still there, but the expression of that gene can be dialed up or down based on outside influences. Interestingly, it is possible to pass these changes through generations. The expression of certain genes within your DNA is not necessarily influenced by the external or internal factors occurring within your lifetime but could rather have been passed down from a lifetime long before your own.

If you have ancestors who lived through a war or plague, the stress and suffering they lived through could very well have triggered epigenetic changes that altered the expression of genes related to anxiety, endurance, or physical health. These epigenetic modifications could have been passed on to your grandparents, then your parents, and then to you.

Most of the research on epigenetics has been conducted on animals, but epigenetic inheritance in humans was brought to public attention by Vivian Rakoff after his research on the children of Holocaust survivors. The research showed that these people, who never directly lived the horrors of the Holocaust, still suffer heightened stress responses and physical changes in their brain structure. The trauma that their parents and grandparents went through has become embedded in their very cells and will likely be passed on to their own children. You can see this in

African Americans, too. They carry transgenerational trauma and epigenetic changes from the brutal realities their ancestors suffered during slavery and systemic racism. These inheritors never stepped foot on a cotton farm 400 years ago, but there are reflections of that suffering encoded in their DNA.

You are just as connected energetically and biologically to your ancestors as you are to your parents. You can fix what they couldn't; you can heal in ways they didn't think they could. You're the latest chapter in a family saga, and you inherited both the gifts and the baggage of your lineage. You don't have to feed the karmic cycles, nor are you bound to the constraints your ancestors faced. They did the best they could with the resources and awareness they had at the time, and now it falls to you. Pick up where they left off, free your lineage, and free yourself.

Universal Law of Cause and Effect

There seems to be an unspoken agreement that karma belongs in the category of spirituality and mysticism. Whoever came up with that idea clearly forgot about the chaos theory, a scientific concept. Chaos theory states that the smallest, most insignificant actions can have huge, unpredictable consequences. It takes it a step further by stating that a butterfly flapping its wings in Brazil can cause a tornado halfway across the world.

Dramatic? Yes.

Does it sound like karma? Also, yes.

Nothing exists in a vacuum. Every decision you make sets off a chain reaction of events that you can't fully anticipate. That interview you decided to go for, the waitress you tipped $20, that habit you picked up - these things snowball in directions you can't predict. That is the law of cause and effect, and karma, to the best of human knowledge, is based on this principle.

Let's paint a picture for you. Imagine it's Tuesday, and you overslept, so you rush out the door and end up getting stuck in terrible traffic. That makes you late for work, which annoys your boss. Your boss, who is now in a bad mood, yells at the cleaning lady, who then goes to the bathroom to cry because she hates her job. While she cries, her sister calls, and she doesn't answer, so her sister assumes something is wrong, panics, and speeds the entire way to check on her because she knows her sister suffers debilitating panic attacks sometimes. As she's flying down the road, distracted and worried about her sister, she runs a red light and T-bones another car in the intersection. The accident leaves both drivers shaken and their cars in no state to be on the road. One of the drivers, a father on his way to drop his kids off at their mom's, is now stuck on the side of the road, desperately trying to find an alternative solution so he can drop his children off safely AND make his flight. This entire scenario occurred because you overslept. The cleaning lady, her sister, the father, his children, and your boss can all trace their current predicament back to that one small decision you made that morning. That is the chaos theory.

The difference between the above example and karma is that in the chaos theory, there is no scientific proof that the action you caused will piggyback onto you, but karma promises it will. Not now, but it definitely will, and so far, it does. Does that make karma an extended version of the chaos theory that science hasn't figured out yet?

Chaos theory shows how unpredictable the universe is, and karma emphasizes your power and responsibility within that unpredictable system. Chaos theory is random and out of control, but karma gives you agency and control. Every time you do something, feel something or think something, you are influencing the future. You are leaving an imprint.

Chaos Theory shows how unpredictable the universe can be.[3]

To put this in perspective, imagine walking down the street and seeing someone drop their wallet. Right then and there, you have a choice: pick it up and return it to them, or you could just keep walking and ignore it. If you choose to return the wallet, you're helping someone, you're being kind, and doing the right thing. That leaves a positive, energetic imprint. The person who dropped the wallet will feel relieved and grateful. They may even pay that kindness forward and do something nice for someone else.

If you decide to keep walking and not return the wallet, or even worse, pick it up and keep it, the person who lost the wallet will be frustrated and upset. They might become cynical about the world and unlikely to trust or help others moving forward. You just left a negative energetic imprint.

It is always your choice, and the effect of whatever decision you make is not a punishment or a blessing. You can choose to see it that way, but all it is, is cause and effect. Karma is cause and effect. Ancestral karma was caused by the actions, emotions, and intentions of your ancestors, and the effects have been tearing through your family tree.

Signs of Inherited Karma

Recurring Family Conflicts

One lineage battling the same relationship issues over and over, generation after generation, is a sign of ancestral karma. There could have been grandparents who were locked in a bitter feud with their siblings until they died, and now the children are in a similar stalemate with their own siblings. The women in your family could be known for judgmental and controlling behavior. There might be unspoken resentments, unaffectionate family members, and a general toxicity that everyone seems to not notice, or maybe they do, but it's so normal that everyone is comfortable with it, except for you. Thankfully, a pattern doesn't have to be your destiny. Karma is cause and effect, not fate.

Financial Struggles

A family could be living in poverty, no matter how hard everyone works. For generations, they've lived paycheck to paycheck. There is so much stress and anxiety around money, and true financial security seems out of reach to them. This is another sign of ancestral karma.

Poverty consciousness is the mindset that there is never enough – not enough money, not enough resources, not enough opportunity. It tells you that abundance is scarce, so you have to fight for every dollar because you're destined to struggle. The thought alone is not the problem; the problem is in the self-sabotaging behaviors it inevitably causes. People with a scarcity mentality are typically impulse spenders. They avoid important money conversations, and they don't save as well as they think.

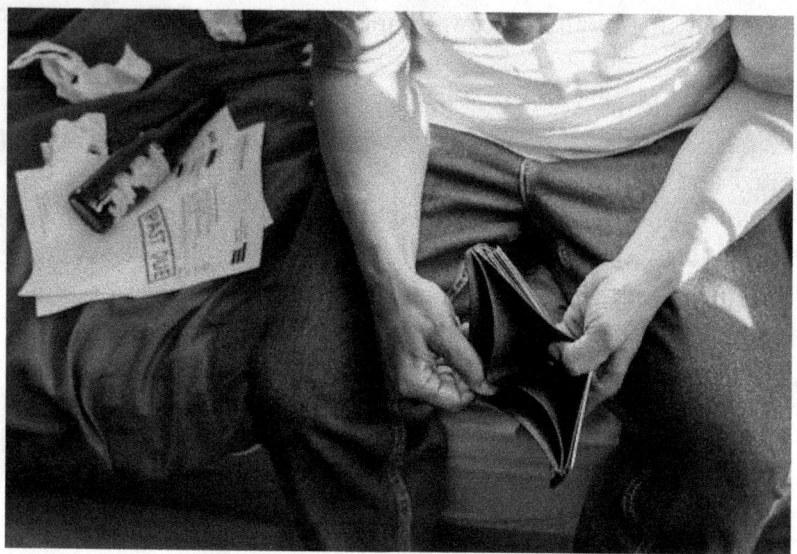

Financial issues can be a result of passed-down habits in lifestyle and spending.[4]

Money habits, money beliefs, and the financial circumstances of your ancestors can find their way down the family tree straight to you. Your great-grandmother may not have had the means to create wealth because of the times in which she was born, but a lot has changed since then – so why does everyone in your lineage seem comfortable with never having enough? A chronic gambler could have descendants with a tendency to overspend, an aversion to saving, or an unhealthy relationship with money. Father, son, uncle, cousins – they're always knee-deep in debt no matter how many times they try to pay them off. These are all signs of ancestral karma.

Health Issues

There are health issues related and unrelated to genetic diseases. They are both hereditary but are of two different causes. The chronic back pain, heart disease, and autoimmune disorders in your family could be symptoms of ancestral karma. Physical symptoms are passed down as easily as psychological and financial ones, but the energetic current carries them as emotions. These emotions are the traumas and imbalances experienced by your ancestors that are somehow lodged in your body and expressed as diseases. The ancestor in question probably didn't have this disease; what they had was the emotional precursor of it and the emotion itself has traveled down the collective field, manifesting as a disease. Your headache might be your great-great-grandmother's lingering grief from losing a child. The blood pressure symptoms could be the stress and anxiety that your father's family suffered for generations.

Modern medicine might manage the symptoms for this generation, but what about your children? What about your brother's children and their children? The energetic imprint is just waiting to manifest in the next generation, and the cycle will continue if nobody asks the right questions and breaks the cycle. Would you not like to be the cause behind preventing these health problems from ever manifesting in your great-grandchildren?

Toxic Relationships

You could have the same relationship tendencies as your father and their father, and as far up the tree as the problem goes. Children learn behaviors by observing their parents, so if you had emotionally distant parents, it wouldn't be a surprise if you turned out emotionally distant yourself. People seem to confuse ancestral karma and learned behavior. Your tendency to attract or gravitate toward toxic relationships might be imprinted in the family lineage, spiritually and energetically, and not by observation and modeling.

You may have watched the women in your maternal line settle for abusive relationships. Your grandmother was enmeshed with your grandfather, trying to fix him and meet his needs at her own expense. Your mom inherited this and would obsessively cater to your emotionally unavailable dad. Now, despite your best efforts to be different, you've noticed you're only attracted to partners who are needy and dependent. The energetic inheritance in your mother's bloodline is the problem.

Karma and Epigenetics

Karma is a spiritual and philosophical belief. Epigenetics is a scientific subject. These are two very different fields that, on the outside, would sooner pop an eyeball than agree on anything, but the fact is, they're both scratching at the same door. Their beliefs have enough intersections that would permit you to say they are connected and not be entirely wrong.

Cellular memory, a scientific fact, means that cells can and do remember the past, including environmental exposures. Every one of these memories is an epigenetic modification, and when you have children, they inherit not only your genetic information but also the epigenetic changes in your DNA.

You could say cellular memory is the biological manifestation of karma. Scientists will probably say that you're wrong, but are you? Science itself has proven that the cell isn't simply a conduit for your genes. It also records and responds to the life you have been exposed to, meaning that the life you live today will one day become, quite literally, the future genetic makeup of your family tree. That is karma made flesh. In fact, epigenetics might just be a biological validation of the karmic principle, specifically ancestral karma.

Exercise 1: Mapping Your Ancestral Patterns

Your family history has the answer to some of the most important questions you've been asking yourself. Buried somewhere in your ancestors' stories are trends and themes that have determined the experiences of your family members up until *you*. This exercise is going to guide you as you sketch out your family tree and closely investigate the lives of your people. It'll be arranged in steps, so don't worry too much about getting lost or feeling overwhelmed. You can stop at any time and pick up where you left off later.

1. **Step 1:** You'll start by drawing your family tree, going back as many generations as you can. If there are gaps, don't worry about it; do the best you can with the information you have access to.
2. **Step 2:** After drawing your family tree, get to know each member of that tree. Ask questions, do your research, and write down any life events, traumas, or stories that stick out. There could've been a grand-uncle who married five times but still died alone or a great-grandparent who was an alcoholic, the same way your dad and sister are. Write down everything you find, including the good bits.
3. **Step 3:** Turn to the relationships in your family tree. Would you say there have been healthy, supportive partnerships in your lineage? Or has there been a history of divorce and conflict?

How did your ancestors handle love, marriage, and family life? Are there tendencies from their time that have seeped into the current generation? Write down the relationship tendencies and the ancestor they belong to.

4. **Step 4:** Your family's health history is the next thing you'll be looking at. Are there shared diseases like heart disease, mental illness, or addiction? Are these illnesses always expressed in the next generation? How much trauma can you find going up your family tree? What kind of trauma, and where are they likely to manifest in the physical body? Do you see a connection between the illnesses of today and the traumas of yesterday? Who in your family tree was traumatized, and how? Write down all their names.

5. **Step 5:** Your family's financial history is another thing you need to check, even if there are no financial problems in your immediate family. How did your ancestors earn money? Were they poor, comfortable, or very wealthy? How would you describe their relationship with money based on whatever information you could find? Are there any financial similarities between your generation and any generation from the past?

6. **Step 6:** Don't forget to check for emotional and psychological patterns. How do you express (or suppress) feelings in your family? Is this consistent with how your ancestors did it? Can you find any dominant personality traits like introversion or optimism that go back generations? Which of these emotional tendencies do you have? Do any of your ancestors share that with you? If there is, you need to find out as much as you can about them.

It might take a while to gather all this information, depending on how much family history you can get your hands on, but when you have all the data you can find, write down your observations, every last one. Get as personal and vulnerable as possible when you compare your findings to your life. Are there any parallels, even the ones you are afraid to admit to yourself? When you look at your ancestors, does it feel like looking in a mirror? What can you learn from their lives? What kind of people were your ancestors?

Exercise 2: Epigenetic Inheritance

For this exercise, you will be looking into your family's epigenetic history, all the way from your immediate family and their traits to your extended family and ancestral lineage. The data you gathered from the first exercise will help you here.

Physical Traits

What are the physical characteristics that stand out in your family? Do you see shared facial features, height, body types, hair color, or birthmarks? Are there any health conditions, allergies, or sensitivities that affect multiple family members? How do you think this relates to your ancestors? Today's digestive issues might come from a time when your ancestors were in survival mode or suffered nutritional deficiencies. Hairy skin may have been necessary for your ancestors to survive in their environment in the past.

Emotional Themes

What emotional tendencies and behavioral predispositions run in your family? Do you all have similar moods, stress responses, or communication styles? Are there emotional wounds, fears, or compulsions that everyone has, even if nobody knows where they came from? Emotional patterns and responses could be grounded in your family's history. Trauma, suffering, or grief that never healed can cause epigenetic changes that then manifest in future generations.

Habits

Write down the habits, lifestyle choices, and coping mechanisms that run in your family. Are there addictions, financial habits, religious/spiritual beliefs, or parenting techniques that are just as repetitive as your family's physical features? Repetitive behaviors, especially negative ones, tend to start as survival strategies, cultural traditions, or coping mechanisms for unprocessed emotions. Generational substance abuse may have started from one ancestor's attempts to self-medicate anxiety or trauma, both of which can trigger epigenetic changes. Perfectionism or workaholism might come from scarcity or insecurity in the family history. You won't know these things if you don't inspect and dive deep into your family tree.

Go through the data you have written down to see if you can find any collective traumas or life circumstances that might have contributed to these patterns or caused them entirely.

Search for:
- Immigration or forced displacement
- Histories of colonization, slavery, or genocide
- Premature losses or deaths in the family
- Persistent poverty, discrimination, or social marginalization
- Childhood abuse, neglect, or other forms of trauma

Using this plethora of information, what traits and tendencies in your family are reflections of these experiences? Apart from you, is anyone else in your family trying to free themselves from this transgenerational trauma? Did any of your ancestors try to break the cycle? What cycles do YOU feel should be broken?

Chapter Two: Tracing the Lineage of Pain and Trauma

"Secrets that are buried long enough become ghosts." - Unknown

When a secret is buried, in this case in a family, the point is to not only hide it from the world but also hide it from the one who buried it. The most elaborate stories are created and told to explain away the uncomfortable truth, and in the process, there is a fragmentation of the person and the family. Inside this tear, something malignant grows, and it spreads its tendrils through the generations, infecting each new branch of the family tree until it is cut out and the wound is sealed.

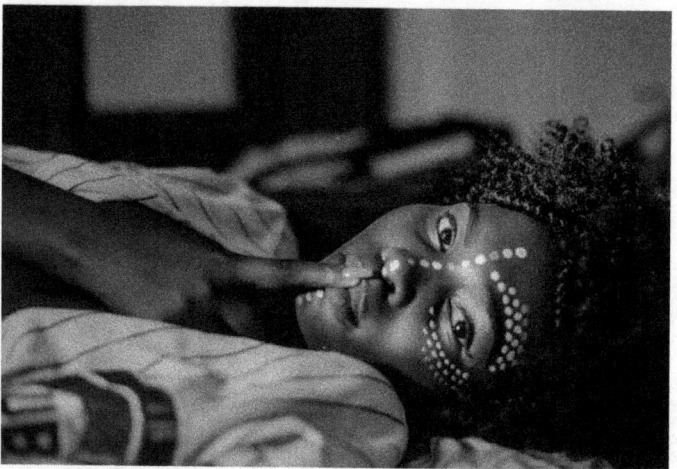

The build-up of hidden truths throughout the ages in your lineage can pile up and affect the way you think and live.⁵

The cultural taboos around several topics – mental health, abuse, infidelity, and death – compel people to keep these wounds hidden, even from themselves. So the secrets accumulate, layer upon layer, each generation adding their own traumas to the ever-growing pile. The family is now infected with blatant lies, half-truths, and unspoken pain.

After experiencing abuse, loss, or betrayal, many families choose to bury these experiences, scared of social stigma and the potential consequences of exposure. Once upon a time, there were topics that couldn't be spoken out loud unless you could risk being shunned, ostracized, or torn apart, especially in smaller communities or cultures where reputation was everything. Generation after generation, families learned to swallow their pain, and silence descended over the most traumatic experiences – domestic abuse, public lynchings, and child molestation. To break the silence was to risk everything, but they were unaware that the silence was costlier, and currently, the generations after them have been paying the price.

Each new child born into these families inherits the grief, rage, and shame of their ancestors. They grow up without a language to articulate this feeling, and subconsciously, they seek out situations that mirror the original wounding, as if their very soul is attempting to finally make sense of it, to find resolution. But there is no resolution without truth.

The Four Kinds of Family Secrets

1. The Deadliest Secrets

The most harmful family secrets are the ones that contain violence or abuse, like murder, sexual abuse, assault, incest, or rape. These secrets are the most damaging because they not only hurt the victims but also create fear, suspicion, and emotional devastation within the entire family. Burying these types of secrets generates karma for the whole family. The victims will suffer PTSD, depression, anxiety, and betrayal, while the family denies these traumatic experiences out of guilt or fear. This silence and denial can be interpreted as permission for the abuse to continue because the victims, too ashamed or scared to speak up, are sitting ducks for the abuser to keep exploiting their power. Victims of these secrets grow up broken, betrayed, and disconnected from their own bodies and emotions. They numb the pain and hide all vulnerability. This coping mechanism is then passed on to their children, who pass it on to the next generation and the one after that.

2. The Dangerous Secrets

The next level of family secrets involves things that are demoralizing and risky – but not necessarily life-threatening. This includes substance abuse, eating disorders, addictions (like sex, love, or gambling), and identity secrets like adoption or paternity fraud. Yes, these secrets have nothing to do with physical harm or criminal activity, but they are just as costly to the family. Substance abuse, for example, generally lands a person in financial trouble, causes mental health disorders, and sometimes, violence. Eating disorders and addictions are treated with shame, control, and isolation. Revealing these secrets is not the easiest because the person keeping the secret doesn't want to be judged or rejected by their family. But keeping them is just as painful and disruptive to the lineage because growing up with an alcoholic father or finding out your father isn't really your father because your mom lied can make many children feel insecure, neglected, and ashamed. They might learn it's safer to walk on eggshells, to hide their feelings, and to put the family's reputation before anything. This survival mode eats into their brain and is passed down through the generations as familial PTSD.

3. The Damaging Secrets

These family secrets include anything that violates freedom or boundaries, though not as severely as the first two categories. Secrets such as these destroy trust and shut down communication. Examples of damaging secrets include family enmeshment (meaning boundaries don't exist in the family), unspoken bitterness, closeted sexual orientation, infidelity, and denying or hiding mental illness or death. Many people don't want to disrupt the family dynamic or be seen as troublemakers, so they either don't ask questions or they bury the secret even deeper. Their descendants absorb the family's unconscious scripts about what can and can't be said, what's acceptable and what's taboo. That then becomes their operating system, even if they haven't a clue where it comes from.

4. The Uncomfortable Secrets

The fourth and final level of family secrets is the least harmful, but they are still unsettling and risky for the person keeping the secret. This includes toxic and cultural shame. In this category, you have things like religious conflict, depression, guilt, body dysmorphia, fear, anxiety, or social awkwardness. These secrets may not carry the same risk of physical, emotional, or relational harm as the other categories, but they still affect a person's self-worth and identity. Toxic shame breeds unworthiness and a reluctance to participate in life, while cultural shame puts up barriers to self-expression and true connection. The space to process and release these emotions may not exist for the person, so they travel down the family line to the many generations that come after.

Loyalty to the Past

Loyalty to the past is very real, and odds are, you may not even realize you're doing it. There's a piece of you that feels compelled to walk the same road as your predecessors, as if you're carrying on a family tradition, even if it's not one you would have chosen for yourself.

Your grandparents could've had to fight to the bitter end to earn a living, so they were penny pinchers, and now YOU are a penny pincher, even though your financial situation is much better. Or your parents might have had a difficult relationship because your dad was chronically unfaithful, and now you are either unfaithful yourself, or you tolerate infidelity in your relationships.

If this is you, your problem is that you might be tethered to the narratives of your ancestors, even if you can't explain why. The WHY is loyalty. You could subconsciously be honoring their sacrifices, validating their stories, and somehow keeping them alive. Or maybe you think you're not "worthy" of something better, that you have to suffer to earn your place in the world just like they did. If nobody has told you before, you don't deserve suffering, and your loyalty to the past is holding you back from living your best life.

A reason people cling to the past is a fear of the unknown. Your ancestors' stories, for all their pain and struggle, are familiar. You know what to expect, even if it's not ideal. Charging into uncharted territory is scarier than settling for a life smaller than the one you want to live. You could be worried about not living up to or surpassing their legacy because of fear of failing in the areas they failed at.

Right on top of this fear, you'll find guilt and obligation. You could feel like you owe it to your parents, grandparents, and other relatives to continue their traditions and walk in their footsteps. Breaking free and doing something different may look like a betrayal, even if, in your heart, you know you want something different.

You can honor your ancestor's legacy by not carrying their burdens.⁶

You shouldn't punish yourself with a burden that is not yours to carry. The pain your ancestors went through is valid, and they didn't deserve to endure what they endured, but that pain does not define your worthiness or determine the life you deserve. Their experiences are part of your story, but they don't have to be your entire story. You can shed this self-imposed penance and stop living like you have to atone for living an easier life compared to theirs. It's not disrespecting their legacy; it's honoring it by living authentically and fully. Your ancestors fought hard to give you a shot at living a better life as compared to theirs, and it would be their honor to watch you dream bigger than they could've imagined. You are worthy, trauma or not.

The Stress Response

Speaking of trauma, trauma causes real, disruptive changes that could last for years or a lifetime, and sometimes all it takes is one traumatizing experience. The minute you are traumatized or extremely afraid, your body goes into the fight-or-flight mode. Fight-or-flight is an ancient survival mechanism that evolved to help us handle immediate threats. Faster than you can blink, your brain signals for the release of stress hormones, specifically adrenaline and cortisol. These hormones give you enough energy to lift a car. They heighten your senses and prepare your muscles to either face the danger or run from it.

This reaction is very useful if you're being chased by a bear, caught in a natural disaster, being physically abused, or encountering a life-threatening position. The problem is that the brain doesn't always know the difference between an actual life-or-death situation and something emotionally traumatizing. The body still goes into that stress response, as intense as it is, even if the threat isn't physically present. This is a chronic activation of the stress response system, and it puts your physical and mental health at risk the longer it continues.

Elevated cortisol levels have been linked to several health issues, including high blood pressure and weakened immunity, anxiety, depression, and memory loss. If this high level persists, changes to the structure and function of the brain itself may occur. Look at the hippocampus, which is the section of the brain responsible for forming new memories and regulating the stress response. It is noticeably smaller in people who went through childhood abuse or some other early-life trauma. It literally shrank.

This shrinkage happens because the hippocampus is extremely sensitive to the effects caused by stress hormones, so when it is flooded with cortisol and adrenaline nonstop, the cells in this region deteriorate and can die off. You need a properly functioning hippocampus because, without it, your brain will not be able to process memories and return the body to its original pre-trauma state.

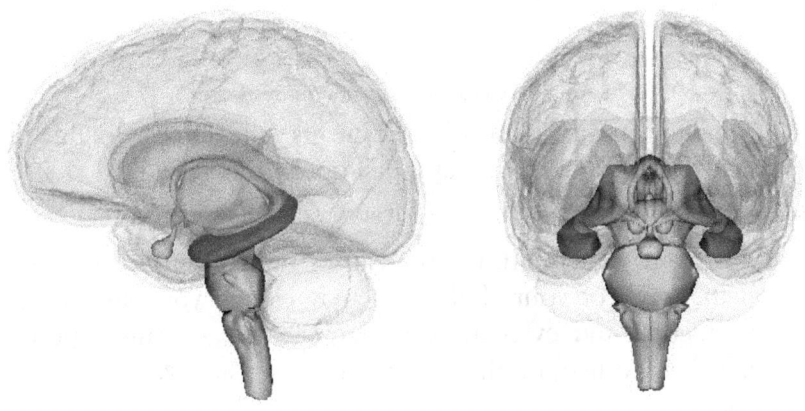

The hippocampus is extremely sensitive to stress hormones.[7]

The amygdala, an almond-shaped brain structure also called the fear center, also suffers from the chronic stress response. It becomes hyperactive, making the person more reactive and sensitive when they perceive a threat, real or imagined. They are either easily startled, can hardly regulate their emotions, feel overwhelming anxiety and anger, or all of the above. These people deserve so much compassion because you don't know what they had to endure for their brain to rewire itself like this. If they don't get the help they need, their brain will stay stuck in survival mode, always on the lookout for danger.

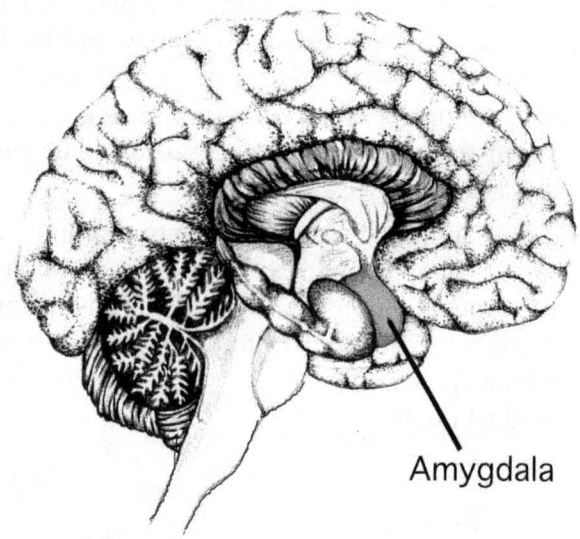

The Amygdala also suffers from stress responses.[8]

Unfortunately, trauma doesn't confine its side effects to the brain. The body feels it, too, in more ways than one:

- **Head**

  Apart from your brain, trauma causes muscle tension in your jaw and the back of your skull. You may clench your jaw and grind your teeth a lot, even in your sleep. That act causes pounding headaches, vertigo, toothache, and tooth sensitivity.

- **Neck**

  All that stress and tension has to go somewhere, and for many people, it ends up right in the neck and shoulders. Tension and restriction in the neck complicate swallowing and neck movement.

- **Back**

    The body likes to store trauma-induced muscle tension in the upper and lower back, but mostly the upper back. Trauma causes knots, spasms, and pain in these areas.

- **Gut**

    Your brain and your gut are tighter friends than you think. If one has a problem, it affects the other. So imagine what happens to your gut while a portion of your brain shrinks. Trauma disrupts the balance that is necessary for the gut microbiome to live, and you need a healthy gut microbiome, or you'll have problems like bloating, constipation, diarrhea, irritable bowel syndrome (IBS), etc. Stress hormones also irritate the lining of the intestines.

- **Immune system**

    Too much cortisol weakens the body's ability to fight infections and diseases, making you more susceptible to colds, flu, autoimmune disorders, etc.

- **Sleep**

    All the stress hormones coursing through your veins are the reason you can't get a good night's sleep. The hyperarousal that comes with the stress response makes it difficult to fall asleep and stay asleep. Some people have nightmares and night terrors, too, as the brain tries to process the trauma during REM sleep.

- **Sexual/Reproductive Health**

    Trauma spares no one, even your most intimate functions. Low libido, sexual dysfunction, menstrual irregularities, and fertility problems are common side effects of a prolonged stress response. The body shuts down these systems to devote resources to survival and self-protection, whether you need it or not.

If all of this is caused by the stress response, you can surely understand how it can play a significant role in epigenetic changes. Your genes are read and expressed fairly consistently, giving you the traits that make you, well, you. So when stress hormones are released, they attach to your DNA and mark certain genes as active or inactive, determining gene expression sometimes up to five generations after the original trauma.

Your ancestors' trauma, your trauma – it's all being recorded and interpreted, and afterward, it is passed on to the next generation. The good news is genetic changes may sound permanent, but they're not. Genetic expression can be retrained and healed. You don't have to live at the mercy of ancient trauma, and neither does the next generation. The road to healing is not magical, but it exists, and it works.

Collective Trauma

Collective trauma is a sensitive subject. There have been too many times in history when humans have suffered unspeakable acts of violence and sheer cruelty at the hands of other humans. Wars, genocides, oppression, and slavery are names that don't even begin to define how horrific these acts were. Entire communities have been scarred, and many of them were wiped off the face of the earth simply for being different. Families were shattered, whole countries stained in blood, by human beings just like them, who bleed and breathe just like them.

It wasn't that long ago, either. There are still children and grandchildren of people who lived through the unspeakable horrors colonization brought to their homes. There are people still alive who witnessed the destruction of their whole life due to war. There are people alive who remember the stories their grandparents told them about whipping posts and cotton farms. Cultural assault like that doesn't just disappear simply because the direct witnesses are no longer alive. Many of their descendants unconsciously carry the ancestral shame and inferiority. You can see it in the disproportionate poverty rates, incarcerations, and health care discrimination in these communities. These people are angry, vulnerable, and filled with resentment.

War survivors were already steeped in anxiety, depression, paralyzing fear, and PTSD after it was announced that the war was over. The war was finally over, but the losses and pain just started. They lost people, property, and safety. They lost their happiness. That trauma doesn't go away when the fighting stops; it stays in the bloodline, it stays in their DNA.

Some communities didn't even survive their war. They were erased by colonization. The colonial powers that ruthlessly subjugated these indigenous populations didn't just seize their land and resources; they also systematically dismantled their culture, tradition, and lifestyle. The damage was not only physical; it was also psychological and spiritual. Generations were forced into residential schools, where they were stripped of their identities and indoctrinated into the colonizers' worldview. Their native languages were suppressed, their religious and cultural practices forbidden, and they were victims of unimaginable physical and sexual abuse. It was a cultural genocide, and not very many people made it out. The ones that did have the memories and consequences engraved in their DNA.

Every one of these wounds runs deep. They are the very real injuries, both visible and invisible, of lineages who survived against all odds. Your lineage survived and will continue to survive, but this time, without the generational trauma. As you read this, know that you walk in the footprints of giants. The blood, sweat, and tears from countless generations before you flow through your veins. You are the manifestation of their refusal to be broken. You are the generational curse breaker.

Signs of Unresolved Generational Pain

Emotional Reactions That Feel Way Over the Top

Are there times when you've gotten upset or angry about something that doesn't warrant such a dramatic reaction? That happens to everyone; it's normal to a degree. It becomes a problem, though, when it happens frequently and for the most trivial reasons. For example, if your partner forgets to do one little chore, you absolutely rain hellfire on them. Or a minor work disappointment has you devastated for days when normally you'd just brush it off. These intense, disproportionate emotional responses could be signs that there are unhealed wounds that have been passed down your family tree. The current trigger is drawing on much older pain that is still swirling around your family's collective energy field, even if you can't pinpoint the exact source. Your body and mind are reacting like the threat is urgent and painful when the reality doesn't match.

Constant, Unexplained Feelings of Guilt, Shame, or Fear

It's common for people dealing with generational trauma to feel haunted by emotions that are hard to ignore but lack an obvious origin. In your case, you might always worry that you're going to ruin things or let people down, even though there's no evidence to suggest that. You could be terribly ashamed of who you are as a person without any clues as to what created those feelings. Hard-to-explain emotions that are anchored in conviction tend to be signs of unresolved pain in your family history.

Struggling to Build Healthy Relationships

It is hard enough carrying generational trauma, not to mention when the trauma threatens to ruin your chances at finding and keeping genuine, healthy relationships. Your trauma might have something to do with trust issues, and so you don't know why you don't trust anyone. You believe they'll hurt or abandon you soon enough, so you leave them first or avoid any relationships at all. Intimacy might feel threatening, so you self-sabotage or pull away from anyone who gets too close. Or you might go the other direction and cling too tightly to relationships because you are terrified of separation and distance. Unhealthy relationship markers like codependency, toxicity, or changing partners, like underwear, are clear signs that you need to heal from generational wounds.

Never Feeling at Home Anywhere

You could live in the neighborhood you grew up in or have lived for an extended period in an area or country far away from your family or childhood home, yet you feel like you never quite belong anywhere. You're always searching for a place to call home, but it somehow eludes you. When your family history is tainted by trauma and displacement, you could feel like you're always on the outside looking in, especially in the places that should feel familiar or like home.

The only way to find out the source of this pain in your lineage is by collecting family stories and asking questions about the past. Sit down with your elders – your uncles, aunties, grandparents, that old woman in your street who sees and knows everything – and respectfully ask them to tell you the stories. Your grandparents may have passed on, but your aunt might know what happened. These stories must be brought to the surface for healing to happen, but be careful; some wounds may still be too raw and painful to share. Don't push it. End the conversation and pick it up later if you must, but these topics must be treated delicately and respectfully. It's all part of the healing process.

Exercise 1: Observing the Trauma Timeline

Gather Information

Reach out to older family members and ask them about the stories in your family history. What were some of the big moments, troubles, or losses that your ancestors experienced? Write down as many details as you can, including dates if possible. You can also dig into any old family documents, photos, or keepsakes you might have access to. These might have clues about your family history.

Create a Timeline

Once you've collected some information, start plotting out a timeline of the significant moments and traumas you've found. If the details are fuzzy, try not to think too much about it; focus on doing your best to reconstruct the sequence of events.

Here are some of the things you might want to include:

- Immigration or migration of your ancestors to a new country/region
- Wars, natural disasters, or other historical events that your family witnessed directly or were affected by
- Illnesses, injuries, or deaths of family members
- Divorces, separations, or other relationship problems
- Financial problems, job losses, debt, or poverty
- Major life transitions like births, marriages, etc.

Recreate the Emotions

As you build your timeline, try to recreate the emotions attached to these moments. What do you imagine your ancestors might have felt? Were they afraid? Was it grief, shame, uncertainty? How do you think these emotions manifested in later generations? How do you think it manifested in you?

Exercise 2: "Follow the Pain" Meditation

1. Take as many deep breaths as you need, then get settled in.
2. Close your eyes if it feels right, or keep them open, whatever works best for you.
3. Scan your body from head to toe, looking out for any areas where you feel tension, irritation, or just pain. Don't judge it or try to fix it; just observe it. You may notice tightness in your shoulders, heaviness in your lungs, or tension in your feet. Wherever you feel that sensation, gently focus your attention there.
4. Breathe deeply as you focus on that spot. Feel the air surrounding the pain. Slowly exhale. Do this three times.

5. What emotion do you think this pain is connected to? Are you sad? Angry? Worried? Sit with that feeling for a minute and be open to any memories, images, or impressions that come to your awareness. As you do that, consider the possibility that this sensation may not necessarily belong to you; it might be linked to one of your ancestors.
6. In your mind, ask, "Whose pain is this? What story does this hide? Which family member could be connected to this feeling?"
7. Keep breathing and wait to see if you sense the presence of the ancestor who owns the pain you feel.
8. If an image or vision comes to you, acknowledge and honor it. If you feel the need to have a conversation with them, go ahead.
9. When you feel ready, place your hand over the area that hurts to recognize and release it. Say to it, "I see you. I honor this pain, and I release it with love."
10. Breathe.
11. Whenever you're ready, open your eyes.

Chapter Three: Uncovering the Family Shadow

According to Carl Jung, the shadow represents the parts of yourself that you don't like or are ashamed of. It's where you stash all the messy, ugly, or socially unacceptable aspects of who you are. Your selfishness, your anger, your biggest fears and insecurities – whatever it is, goes into the shadow. The shadow is everything you'd rather not look at or admit to.

The Shadow Self represents the parts of you that are hidden.'

The shadow develops early on as children. From a young age, you pick up on societal norms and cultural expectations about how you "should" behave. You quickly learn which parts of yourself are acceptable and which are not. For example, suppose you were told that being emotional or aggressive was bad. In that case, that part of you gets hidden away in your shadow.

As you age, these disowned traits and impulses become your shadow - the unknown or forbidden side of your personality that exists underneath the surface of your conscious identity. The shadow is the closet where you keep all your skeletons.

Your shadow isn't good or bad per se; it just contains parts that you haven't fully accepted or integrated yet. Jung saw the shadow as a necessary and critical component of the human psyche, one that needs to be explored and integrated if you want to become your fullest, most authentic self. Jung believed it is necessary to make peace with the shadow.

The shadow manifests through projection. If you have ever met someone who just irritates you for no reason, chances are, they embody some parts of yourself you don't like. You're staring at some aspect of your shadow, and it is staring right back at you.

People make it a habit to accuse other people of having the very qualities that they secretly have but refuse to acknowledge that they are present within themselves. You call your coworker selfish when, if you're being honest, you know you always think of putting your needs first. Or you think your partner is lying when that's something you know you do, too. Projection is how you avoid facing your shadow by pinning those undesirable traits on someone else. It seems like a convenient defense mechanism, except it doesn't change the truth, which is why you lash out at people for having flaws that you won't admit you also have.

The shadow also appears in dreams where there is no conscious control. That's why you have some dreams with confusing, disturbing, or taboo symbolism that represents things you might be too afraid to acknowledge. A dream about quitting your job could be symbolism for your secret wish to be free of your family and do something new. It's symbolism because, in the real world, you may not even have a job at the moment. A dream about violence could be a glimpse into your repressed aggression. These shadow elements appear in your dreams because the dream world lets you bypass your waking censorship straight to your subconscious.

Jung believed that confronting and integrating the shadow is a MUST. He saw shadow work as a necessity for individuation. You can only be whole when you accept all the different pieces of yourself. Integrating the shadow means admitting your dark impulses and flaws instead of disowning or projecting them onto others. You must be willing to look at the parts of yourself that you find ugly, shameful, or unacceptable and make peace with them. It is one of the hardest things to do as a human being. It is scary and humbling to face your worst fears and insecurities, but Jung believed that the rewards outweigh the discomfort. Your shadow contains power and energy that is locked and forgotten. With access to all that power trapped in your unconscious, you get to really live, free from the influence of your muted impulses, free to be all of you.

Integrating your shadow makes you more human, not less. Your creativity, passion, and confidence may be buried in your shadow - power that you have been too afraid to touch. There is more than enough space for the light and the dark, the conscious and the unconscious. There is enough space for you.

The Family Shadow

Families are complicated, messy, and, on many occasions, downright dysfunctional. No matter how much you love your people, there's always something - that tension, those rules, the skeletons in everyone's closet - that makes family relationships the trickiest part of the human experience. This "something" that lurks in the darkness is the family's shadow, and every family has a shadow.

The family shadow is especially potent. That's because families are where you first learn about yourself - where you develop your basic identity. It's the crucible in which your personality is forged, for better or for worse.

Children consume messages from their parents and guardians about what's acceptable and what's not. They quickly learn which parts of themselves are met with love and approval and which parts get shut down, shamed, or pushed away. Soon enough, most of those unacceptable qualities form your individual shadow.

You may have grown up in a home where anger and aggression were seen as unforgivable, so you evolved to stifle your rage, to smile and nod even when you were seething inside. Or it could be that your family valued quiet, obedient compliance, so there was no room for you to be anything but quiet and compliant.

Whatever the case, the shadow that gets banished from your family's consciousness doesn't go anywhere. It's only locked away, but it resurfaces as toxic behavior, for example, through passive-aggression, explosive outbursts, depression, addiction, and so on.

The shadow is the black sheep of the family, the family secret, the elephant in the room that no one wants to talk about. It's the uncle who always causes a scene at Thanksgiving, the sister who's just so sensitive, the father who does a little too much. It's the behaviors, traits, and tendencies that get labeled as bad or wrong and shunted off to the side.

And, of course, families will project their individual shadow onto each other. That's why tensions sometimes arise quickly when relatives get together. Everybody is pushing everybody's buttons, old resentments are coming up, and people are saying things they'll regret later. This is the shadow. When they meet face to face with the disowned parts of themselves through family members, they lash out, they withdraw, they point fingers - anything to avoid having to face their own darkness.

There was this girl, Draya, from three years ago. It was a wedding party. The drinks were flowing, and everyone was either laughing or dancing until Draya's aunt made a comment about her weight. At that moment, you could see Draya`s whole face flood with rage at what some would call a relatively innocent comment. But those closest to Draya knew that she had insecurities about her body - insecurities that she had been trying to keep firmly in the shadows. She ended up yelling at her aunt and storming out of the party. The emotions she had tried so hard to repress just erupted, and she was powerless to control them. Her aunt publicly said something that Draya had said to herself 100 times over - *BUT in secret.* That's the shadow at its most volatile.

The shadow isn't just released in dramatic family blow-ups. It is also expressed more subtly, in pervasive ways that define the entire family dynamic. A good example is the family system where one child is cast as the Golden child while another is relegated to Scapegoat. The golden child is the one who personifies all the family's idealized qualities - they're the smart one, the successful one, the one who makes the parents proud, the good child. Meanwhile, the scapegoat is the one who takes on all the family's shadow material. They're the troubled ones, the black sheep, the ones who can't do anything right.

This system allows the rest of the family to disown their personal flaws and project them onto the scapegoat. The scapegoat becomes the receptacle for everything the family deems unacceptable, from addiction to mental illness to criminality. As expected, this dynamic is plain toxic, both for the scapegoat and for the family as a unit.

The saddest part is that the scapegoat would often internalize this "bad" label to the point where they start to believe they really are the problem. Can you blame them? They become trapped in the role that their family has assigned them, unable to break free and show the world (and themselves) the full complexity of their character.

The shadow in families isn't always as extreme as the scapegoat dynamic, of course. Sometimes, it's just an unspoken rule that particular topics are off-limits. Perhaps you just know to never talk about money, mental health, or the family secrets that everyone knows but pretends they don't in your family setting.

For cases like these, the shadow presents as a heavy silence, an energetic emptiness where the truth is supposed to be. It's the proverbial elephant that no one dares to point out. However, this silence is just as bad as overt dysfunction because genuine connection and intimacy can never take root in secrecy.

How to Recognize the Family Shadow

- **Secrets:** All families have their secrets – the shameful, scandalous incidents that get buried and never spoken of again. For some, it's infidelity; for others, it's addiction or an actual crime. These taboo topics are tossed into the family's shadow, and the longer they are kept under lock and key, the more power they accrue. The shame, guilt, and paranoia surrounding them grow, generating an energetic charge around these forbidden subjects. Families will usually go to great lengths to maintain the illusion and avoid any mention of the secret. But it doesn't matter how hard they try to repress it; it has already made a home in their collective energy field, and so it holds influence. You'll find its influence in the way the family communicates, in how they don't trust each other, how often they tell unnecessary lies, and in the things they are willing to do for their public image.

- **Generational Abuse, Neglect, or Abandonment:** Trauma and dysfunction always find their way to the next generations. If your grandmother was emotionally distant and unavailable, it may have created a longing and disconnection in your dad. Or if your grandfather physically abused your mother, you may have grown up in fear and hypervigilance for no obvious reason. These generational traumas live on in the family's collective psyche and show up in their relationships, mental health, and toxic behaviors. The family may be repeating the same dysfunctional behaviors and may be unable to imagine living any other way.

- **Emotional Repression:** For many families, the shadow is emotional repression. There was no announcement, but everyone knows that feelings are off-limits or unacceptable. Affection and vulnerability could've been strictly taboo once upon a time in the lineage, and every display of emotion was punished. Or the family has never been able to express love and care in big ways, in healthy ways. This emotional constriction became part of the family's shadow, influencing their interpretation of connection and intimacy. There is a disconnect between them, and members of this lineage feel isolated, unseen, and misunderstood.

- **Shame Around Identity:** Another potent family shadow material comes from the shame and stigma that can be attached to a person's identity or background, like if your grandparents immigrated to this country and had to change their names to fit in. Or if your family has always been looked down upon by the local community because you belong to the lower class. These shouldn't be sources of shame, but they are, and as you know, everything shameful goes into the shadow. Now, there could be descendants who hate themselves, descendants who always feel out of place, descendants who go the extra mile to overcompensate for being "less than," descendants who are ashamed of their heritage and would rather never discuss it. They carry a shame that is not even theirs.

- **Shame Around Sexuality:** Sexuality has always been a prickly topic in society, but now more than ever. This shadow around sexuality can take many forms. Your family could have a hush-

hush rule that you don't talk about sex, period. There could be irritation around LGBTQ+ identities. It could even be something as simple as an expectation that you'll follow a sexual script - get married, have kids, etc. - without any space for deviation. The relatively mainstream heterosexuality is still shamed and suppressed in some families today. Parents have reacted in anger and disgust after finding out that their daughter was sexually active. The girl, growing up, may have internalized the message that girls are dirty or promiscuous for having sex, while boys are champions for doing the same thing. Sexual shame hides in the background of many family shadows, and so many people are forced to choose between their authenticity and their family's acceptance.

Passing the Shadow to the Next Generation

Emotional Suppression By Parents/Caregivers

More often than not, the shadows that get passed down to the next generations are caused by unhealed pain, trauma, or grief that the previous generation was unable or unwilling to fully confront. Examples are parents or grandparents who never healed from the loss or abuse in their childhood. Life probably forced them to bury those emotions for survival reasons. In place of working through their pain, they came up with coping mechanisms like emotional detachment, stoicism, or control, and then, without realizing it, modeled those same avoidant behaviors for their children, who in turn modeled it for their children, too. The message then becomes: Feelings are dangerous. Don't show weakness. Just keep going.

Parents and caregivers can instill the habit of holding back emotions.[10]

Behavioral Patterns as Coping Mechanisms

Behavioral patterns and coping mechanisms also form the family's intergenerational shadow. Behaviors like perfectionism, control issues, or emotional detachment are an attempt to manage the anxiety, shame, or fear that comes from lingering family problems. Collin had an alcoholic, emotionally abusive man for a grandfather. In response, his father was a rigid, perfectionistic disciplinarian who demanded flawless academic and athletic performance from his children. To Collin's father, if you're not perfect, you're unlovable. Collin dealt with inadequacy all his life. He became a workaholic and always pushed himself to the brink of burnout. He was afraid to fail, and so he did everything in his power to avoid the shame and rejection he had witnessed in his family's past. This was the emotional legacy he inherited.

Silent Agreements and Unspoken Family Rules

"This is just how it is." "Don't say it again." "Leave it alone." You may have heard any or all of these sayings several times. It's these statements that reprogram the family's collective consciousness. Everyone knows never to talk about Uncle Barry's cocaine problem, mom's affair, the fact that Camille ran away, or anything that has to do with spending money. These are only examples of taboo topics ingrained in your family – the ones nobody talks about as if they had never happened. The logic is if something has been buried and denied for long enough, it might as well be just the way things are. That logic is harmful.

The Cost of Avoiding the Family Shadow

Isolation and Loneliness

Ignoring the family shadow turns you into an observer, disconnected from the same people and emotions that should feel the most familiar. There should be closeness and support from the people you love, but in its place, there is disconnection and loneliness. Everybody has to tiptoe on eggshells in fear of their authenticity. Nobody wants to open old wounds, and so they choose the safer option: emotional distance. You see the familial bond that other families have, and you want that, but you're okay with being adrift in a sea that should be love because the family agrees that shadow should stay in the shadows.

Mental Health Issues

If you've ever tried to hold your breath underwater, you would hope you could stay there forever; however, sooner or later, you're going to come up gasping for air. Those disagreements that get swept under the rug, the anger that nobody is allowed to express, the unaddressed traumas – they seep into the psyche and destroy everything they touch. You could be drowning in anxiety, depression, or PTSD-like symptoms while your mind works overtime to process the shadow you've been trying to ignore. You might say to yourself, "It's too mentally and emotionally draining to show up as your best self in the world," and the worst part is, the more you try to convince yourself that you can do this forever, the more it feels like you can't.

Physical Illnesses

Your physical body is a perfect mirror of your emotional body, and each time you suppress or ignore the shadows within your family, you create emotional blockages that are reflected in your physical health. Your cells remember the tension and stress from three generations ago, let alone the ones from your lifetime. These memories show up as seemingly unrelated symptoms. The headaches you've been getting could be a mirror of the anger you never let out. Your constipation might be untreated depression. You could wake up with chronic muscle pain or autoimmune disorders because your body is begging you to look at the shadow that is clearly affecting you so much. Don't hesitate to get the medical help you need, but sometimes, it's only your body telling you something your mind has been trying to tell you for weeks or years.

Strained Relationships

Every so often, to ignore the family shadow means to ignore the family. You can't have conversations with your family like you used to because you can't open up and be yourself. You realize you're holding back so much and are afraid to say the truth or, at the very least, your truth. And when you do try to communicate, it's just as effective as speaking a completely different language because the shadow wants to stay hidden. This breakdown in communication slowly erodes your closest relationships until everyone can see that you have drifted so far away from the very people who should be in your corner. Neither of you can see the wall, but if you reach out, you can touch it.

Missed Opportunities for Growth

You can only stumble around for so long in a dark room, so why not just turn on the lights? You risk bumping into things the longer you stay in the dark, but more importantly, you're missing out on the chance to see what's in front of you. For every difficult conversation you choose not to have, you deny yourself the opportunity to grow and heal. You're choosing to stay in the dark, to forfeit the maturity and self-awareness that could come from healing yourself from the shadow. Growth doesn't happen in safe spaces. The path of least resistance might be easier, but the cost is your potential.

Regardless of how important it is to face and heal your family's shadow, you have to lead with empathy, or it will all be for nothing. Pointing fingers and pushing blame does nothing to help the work you're trying to do. It only makes everyone want to shut down and protect themselves. You have to make space for the healing to happen, and it won't happen under judgment. You don't fight darkness with swords and armor; you fight it with light.

Exercise 1: Shadow Genogram

1. Take a pen and paper and write down everything you know about your family history. Talk to your parents, grandparents, and other older relatives. See what stories, memories, and information they can give you. Go through old photos and documents if you have access to them.
2. Pay attention to births, deaths, and major life changes, but most importantly, to the emotional undercurrents and relational nuances that thread through the generations. Was there a narcissistic grandparent who always played the victim? Have there been any addicts in your family? Has there been a sibling who was scapegoated or shunned by the family?
3. These are the details that expose the shadow themes that may have tormented your family for generations.
4. Look for anyone afraid of vulnerability, the perfectionists in the family – or the avoidants in the family. Whatever you find, write it down because these are the emotional breadcrumbs that will help you understand your family's shadow.

5. Once you have all your information, you'll need a genogram. Draw a basic family tree, going back at least three generations, if you can. Include all the key players - parents, grandparents, aunts, uncles, siblings, etc. It doesn't have to look fancy; you're drawing a map, not a Leonardo da Vinci painting.
6. While you're assembling this family tree, start annotating it with the events, emotional states, and habits you discovered in your research. Was there a loss that was never properly grieved? A parent who was emotionally or physically abusive? A sibling rivalry that lasted until they both died?
7. Try to decode the silent agreements, too - addiction, mental health, infidelity, rape, and so on. These silent agreements are equally important to the family shadow. There could be prevalent anxiety and stress among the women in your family, all of which you now learned come from your great-grandmother. She was expected to be the picture-perfect wife with seven children while she also managed the household and cared for her elderly parents. She never had the chance to sit with or process any feelings she had about her life, so she convinced herself that her feelings didn't matter. That then became the expectation for all the women who came after her. That is the reason for the anxious, high-strung tendencies in you and other women in your lineage.
8. Another shadow example is emotional distance and disconnection. There could be uncles in your family tree who were physically present but emotionally unavailable, aunties who saw affection and vulnerability as signs of weakness. Following that thread, you might learn that it comes from your grandfather, who grew up in a home that didn't tolerate emotion, so he had to toughen up. That "toughen up" mentality became a silent agreement in the family lineage.
9. After you finish with the genogram, look at your family tree as a whole. Many more things will make sense when the picture is complete. This genogram contains the origin of your family's emotional inheritance - the shadow that no one dares look at, no matter how dysfunctional it may be.

Exercise 2: Excavating the Family Shadow

This is an exercise in honesty and vulnerability. It looks easy, but it's not. Not completely. For this exercise, all you need to do is talk. You'll be playing 20 questions with as many relatives as you can.

Your area of inquiry is entirely up to you, but here are a few suggestions:

- "What are some of your earliest memories growing up in our family?"
- "I've always wondered, what was your relationship like with your parents and grandparents?"
- "Were there any family traditions or rituals that were really important when you were young?"
- "I heard a rumor about so-and-so. Is there any truth to that story?"
- "What were some of the biggest problems or hardships the family faced when you were a child?"
- "Do you remember any funny or embarrassing family stories?"
- "Were there any family members who were considered 'black sheep' or lived rebellious lives?"
- "What were your parents' and grandparents' relationships like?"
- "What were some of the happiest or most meaningful moments the family shared together when you were young?"
- "Were there any family myths, superstitions, or spiritual beliefs that were important when you were growing up?"
- "Do you know anything about how our ancestors ended up in this part of the world?"
- "Were there any family members who served in the military or lived through a war?"
- "What kind of future did your grandparents think the family would have?"
- "Are there any family heirlooms, photos, or keepsakes that are special to you?"

- "What were some of the hardest lessons the family had to learn over the generations?"

Not every topic will be discussed, at least not immediately. Don't push for any details your family isn't ready to share, but know the difference between not wanting to have a painful conversation and keeping a secret. Bringing the shadow into the light is the first step to healing it.

Exercise 3: Recognizing Your Family Shadow

This exercise is here to help you increase your awareness of your shadow within the greater family shadow. These are your unconscious behaviors and responses around your relatives. They are the side of you that interacts with and contributes to the collective family shadow.

Here's how to unpack this:

1. Concentrate on your emotions whenever you're with family members. Anytime you feel that familiar discomfort, defensiveness, or any other strong reaction around your family member, write it down immediately or make a mental note to do it later. It could be how your sister makes a sly comment about your outfit that gets to you – or how your dad sighs whenever you bring up your career. Watch out for these moments and how you feel during or after them. Don't let the feeling wash over you, and then move on. Sit in it, not to stew, but to understand what's happening inside you. Does it make you feel tension? Where in your body do you feel it? Is your heart racing? Do you want to shut down or lash out? Your physical and emotional responses matter.

2. Ask yourself some questions. What happened right before I felt this way? What need or desire wasn't being met? How do I typically respond when I feel this way – do I withdraw, explode, or do something else? For example, your brother could've made a joke about your cooking, and almost immediately, you felt like a failure. If you question those feelings, it could be that you just want to be appreciated for your efforts in the kitchen, and nobody does. Or your mom's incessant nagging about your single status makes you feel inadequate, and all you would like is her approval. Don't settle for the first answer your mind gives you; that's a surface-level explanation. Go deeper, ask yourself the

hard questions.

3. Write it all down in a journal. The more details, the better – what was said, who was involved, how your body felt when it happened. This written record will show you the patterns in your behavior. Journaling forces you to slow down and understand what happened. You don't need to write a novel; just a few sentences or bullet points will do. As long as it is a documented reference of your trigger moments, you're well on your way to understanding your shadow.

4. Go back to your journal and look for the common denominators. Are there particular family members, topics, or situations that have, on more than one occasion, been your emotional hot buttons? What do these situations tell you about your family's issues or unmet needs? You may notice that you always get defensive when your dad compares you to your high-achieving siblings. Or you realize that you zone out whenever your in-laws start asking when you and your partner are going to have children. Triggers like these point to wounds that need healing in yourself and in the family.

5. Knowing what you know, do you think you'll respond differently next time? What exactly will you do differently? Do you think there are healthier ways to express those feelings or discuss the root causes? What are those ways, and are you open to using them? This is not to completely eliminate your triggers; that's likely impossible, but you can work on developing more self-awareness and healthier coping mechanisms. Maybe next time your sister throws a comment about your clothes, you breathe first and then respond with vulnerability, not defensiveness. Or when your mom starts complaining, you set a boundary and kindly but firmly ask her to stop. Intentional responses are always more effective than autopilot reactions.

Exercise 4: Meeting The Family Shadow

1. Go to a quiet, comfortable space where you can sit undisturbed. Breathe in deeply as your body settles and your mind becomes focused.

2. Close your eyes and imagine your family tree appearing as an actual tree.

3. See the tree trunk in your mind's eye and feel it grounding you in the present. Imagine the branches stretching up into the sky and back through generations of your ancestors.
4. Imagine that the tree can speak to you; imagine that it is alive. Ask the tree to reveal a family shadow that is ready to be seen and healed.
5. Don't try to control the response. Stay open to whatever wants to come through. You could receive an image, a memory, or a feeling. Trust that whatever comes to you is exactly what you need to know right now.
6. While you listen and observe, watch the tree closely. Do you see a twisted branch? A section of the trunk that looks damaged or decayed? Do you feel heaviness or sadness coming from the tree?
7. Try not to judge or analyze whatever you notice; feel it instead. This is a sensitive process; it needs to be treated with curiosity and compassion.
8. The image or sensation you get might be faint, but that doesn't mean you should dismiss it. Sometimes, the quietest shadows carry the most powerful lessons.
9. If you get a strong or intense hit, that's okay too. Hold space for it. Don't try to push it away or change it. Here, you're the observer, not the critic.
10. When you're finished, open your eyes and get your journal. Write down everything you saw, heard, and felt during the visualization.
11. Think about what your observations mean and which family shadow they might represent. How does it connect to your life, beliefs, or habits? What issues or karma does it point to within your family history?
12. Always approach your investigations compassionately, for your and your family's sake. The shadow isn't a weakness or a flaw; it's everything that has been ignored for far too long and left to pile on top of each other.
13. When you feel ready, write a statement in your journal saying what you intend to do with this newfound awareness. Mean it as a promise to yourself more than anything. The statement could

sound something like this: "I'll explore this shadow with courage and compassion, bringing healing to my family line. I hold space for the pain and struggle, but I also see the determination and strength in my lineage. I am committed to breaking free from unhealthy cycles and to creating a new, healthier legacy for myself and future generations."

14. This declaration will be a reminder of your intention as you continue to unravel and hopefully heal your family shadow.

Chapter Four: The Call to Healing: Preparing for the Journey

Crisis and disruption are the two things that can guarantee a wake-up call. They strip away any distractions and illusions that are clouding your mind to the truth, and they don't do it gently. You're forced to confront reality raw and unfiltered. All those feelings you've been shoving down – the fear, the anger, the sadness – they get dragged out into the open. It's uncomfortable, and your first instinct will probably be to make it stop, to get everything under control again, but sometimes, things must fall apart for them to come together again, this time, to create something better.

The healing journey starts with you confronting the past.[11]

It's human nature to want order and stability. You build routines, make plans, and convince yourself that you're in control, but life is inherently chaotic, and you know this. Try hard as you might; there will always be times when the rug gets pulled out from under you. But what if this crisis is actually a blessing in disguise? What if the upheaval you're desperately trying to fix is the necessary catalyst for your transformation? It's so tempting to see disruption as something to be avoided at all costs, but what if you try to build something brand new, replacing the old version of yourself instead of trying to put the pieces back together exactly as they were?

Survival instincts are the reason people cling to the known, even when the known is no longer of use or rather detrimental to them. It's not their fault; the human brain is wired for self-preservation; it's an evolutionary adaptation that served primitive humans well when their world was crawling with real threats. Today's dangers are more abstract - job insecurity, relationship issues, mental health disorders - and yet, the brain still reacts the same, especially when the only way forward is to fully surrender to the chaos and let things fall apart completely.

Buried under the chaos, the tears, the confusion, the recurrent cycles, the betrayal, the toxic relationships, and occasionally, the medical issues are old wounds you need to heal. Healing may be emotional as you work through ancestral emotions and traumas. It may be mentally related as you reframe the distorted thoughts that didn't begin with you in the first place. It may be physical, as you discover how trauma, ancient or not, has manifested in your body. Finally, it will definitely be spiritual as you reconnect with your authenticity, heal your lineage, and find meaning in the chaos.

Recognizing the Need for Healing

Answer these questions honestly, and don't worry if most of your answers are YES. It's a good sign if they actually are. It means you're in touch with your inner shadows that are calling for your attention and healing. This isn't to diagnose or label you but to increase your awareness and understanding. Where you go from here is completely up to you.

- Do you ever feel like you carry a darkness or burden that you can't explain?
- Have you noticed dysfunctional cycles that repeat throughout your lineage?

- Do you sometimes feel out of place or disconnected from your family's culture or traditions?
- Do you feel loss or mourning for suffering you never got to experience?
- Are you extremely protective of your lineage?
- Are there any unhealthy coping mechanisms (like addiction) shared by more than one generation?
- Do you feel shame, guilt, or unworthiness that you can't trace back to a source?
- Is it hard to trust outsiders or let your guard down, even in safe relationships?
- Do you ever feel like you're living out a script or destiny that was predetermined for you?
- Have you experienced physical symptoms like chronic pain or illness that don't have a clear medical cause?
- Generally speaking, do you lack joy, purpose, or satisfaction in your life?
- Can you effectively communicate your needs and boundaries with your family?
- Do you ever feel that your financial problems or instability are inescapable?
- Do you take on more responsibilities than you can reasonably handle?
- Do you self-sabotage or undermine your progress?
- Do you always feel like an outsider or like you don't belong anywhere?
- Can you set healthy boundaries with demanding or controlling family members?
- Do you receive emotional support or nurture from your family?
- Do you see a future for your lineage that is not dictated by your family's past?
- Do you feel the compulsion or obligation to fix your family's problems?

- Would you say you're in control of your life?
- Do you trust or have faith in institutions, systems, or authority?

Signs to Uncover and Heal Ancestral Wounds

Recurring Patterns

These patterns are repetitive no matter what you do or how hard you try to free yourself. You've tried and failed to think your way out of these situations. It could be your tendency to attract the same types of friends over and over again - the friends who are manipulative or destiny swappers. It could be the way you manage money. Somehow, you're always in debt despite your best efforts to get it together. Repetitive themes are frustrating and confusing, especially when they don't seem to make any logical sense. But they don't make sense because you're looking for answers in the wrong places. Recurring patterns are either karmic or ancestral, and to break the cycle, you need to find its source. This is a problem with your subconscious, and that is why you unknowingly recreate those same patterns as your ancestors. Their stories, to a degree, are embedded in your subconscious, so you're enacting a play written long before you were born. In a way, these generational wounds are asking to be healed, or you will keep getting cast in the same role over and over again.

Intuitive Nudges

The signs of ancestral wounds aren't always noticeable or 3-dimensional. Sometimes, all you get is a feeling, a persistent thought or image, a gut feeling that something important is being overlooked or avoided. These intuitive nudges are your subconscious trying to direct your attention to the places that need to be healed. Your intuition is more connected to the energetic currents in your lineage, even when your conscious mind has no idea what's going on. Honoring these intuitive messages can grant you access to information you didn't even know existed. It could be recurring dreams about an ancestor you never knew or a nudging inner call to research your family lineage more than ever. These are the breadcrumbs that your psyche is leaving for you, and all you need to do is follow them.

Emotional Resonance

It's not strange for an emotion to hit out of nowhere, like feeling grief all of a sudden, or unexplainable fear, or heaviness that you can't shake. If it happens to you, trust that it happens to many more people as well.

It's just that only a few of them try to figure out why. These out-of-the-blue emotions are often signs that you briefly plugged into the pain and trauma carried by your ancestors. It truly is a disorienting and uncomfortable feeling; it is as if you want to cry for no reason, but instead of rationalizing it or shutting it down, have compassion for it and for yourself. This is part of the healing process.

Recurrent Dreams

Dreams are a portal into the unseen, a gateway to the mysterious and unknown spaces in your mind. If you're having recurring dreams about family members, ancestors, or symbolic imagery that you intuitively feel is connected to your family history, don't ignore it. Your dreams are trying to reveal something important about the ancestral narratives and energies that influence your life with or without your awareness.

Dreams are your portals into the unseen parts of your mind.[12]

Messages from Your Ancestors

Ancestors love to stay connected to their descendants long after they are gone. They obviously can't come out and talk to you directly, but they come up with creative channels to share their stories, their wisdom, and, not to mention their desire for healing.

One of these creative channels is signs and synchronicities. Ancestors try to reach out through the little signs and synchronicities that keep showing up in your life. You've noticed a particular animal, object, or color showing up again and again, so much that you could say it's following you around. Or a song, phrase, or image might catch your attention every time, even when you're not looking for it. These repeating symbols and coincidences are a trail that your ancestors have left for you to find. They could be trying to get your attention because they want to show you something significant from their lives, or they want to point you towards a family wound or cycle that needs to be addressed and healed.

Signs and synchronicities are effective because the same sign can mean ten different things to ten different people. When you see a sign, the first thing you need to do is ask what it means to you. Forget about generic interpretations, and don't take another person's interpretation at face value. Connect with your intuition and ask, "What does this remind me of? What feelings or memories do I get from this?" The minute you get an answer from your own heart and soul, the sign's job is done.

Your ancestors can also reach out to you in your dreams. The veil between the world of the living and the spiritual realm is thinnest in the dreamscape, so it is one of the few places you can receive messages from beyond the physical realm. Your ancestors know this, so they use it to send messages directly or encode them in symbolism.

Through these dream visions, your ancestors can share important lessons, expose buried truths, or assist with much-needed healing. If you see an ancestor's old home, for instance, a place they know you will recognize from photos or descriptions, it could be a message to investigate the intergenerational patterns and cultural legacies that originated within those walls. Or a mythic dream sequence could show you the trauma, loss, and rebirth your lineage has experienced.

Dream messages require receptivity. Don't try to overanalyze or interpret them too literally. Rather, concentrate on the emotions, the symbols, and your intuitive wisdom on what's being communicated. Your ancestors won't send you a pointless message that you can't decode. So, if you don't understand it immediately, give it time; it'll come to you. The answer is already inside of you.

Ancestors also communicate through spontaneous realizations, epiphanies, and direct spiritual encounters. You could be going about your day when suddenly, an energetic download that is just too vivid rushes through your mind, or you get a random understanding of a story in your family history. Sometimes, you could even feel a powerful, energetic presence during your meditation, as if an ancestor is right there watching over you.

Any mystical encounter is moving and life-changing, but ancestral ones remind you that your ancestors aren't really gone – they live on in the energy, the stories, and the unfinished business that still exists in your family tree. And it is through these direct spiritual communications that they're able to share valuable pieces of information in hopes that it will help you heal the family and carry on a better legacy.

How Is the Family/Ancestral Line Healed?

- **Shamanic Journeying:** Shamanic journeying is a sacred meditation practice where you enter a state of heightened awareness to connect with your ancestral lineage. On these journeys, there will be clear communication with your ancestors. People have received images, symbols, and sounds that they know are connected to their family's history. They have received life-changing wisdom, guidance, and healing energy directly from their ancestors.

- **Ancestral Rituals:** Performing ceremonies and rituals that honor your ancestors keeps you connected to your roots and helps heal familial wounds. Ancestral rituals could involve setting up an ancestral altar with sentimental items, lighting candles, reciting prayers or chants, or simply making time to pay respects and connect with the souls from previous generations. Rituals allow you to express gratitude, ask for favors, and create a sacred space for your ancestors to be present. It's a family reunion, of sorts, but with ancestral spirits. The Disney animation Coco is a perfect example of this.

- **Forgiveness:** Clinging to resentment and blame, carrying anger in your heart towards yourself, your ancestors, or other family members can block any and every healing process. Nothing grows in bitterness, and anger is too heavy a burden to give to the next generation. Forgiveness is the way out – forgiveness for yourself and everyone in your lineage. To forgive, you may need to write a letter. You may need to have difficult conversations or simply feel compassion for the mistakes your ancestors made in the past – compassion for them and whoever they wronged. You can acknowledge the pain that your family has caused or faced while also acknowledging that everyone is doing what they can with what they have. Forgiveness is not an excuse; it is simply the key to peace and freedom.

- **Symbolic Acts of Closure:** People seek closure because it is how they move on, process their emotions, and find peace. You may need closure for yourself or on behalf of an ancestor who never got the chance. This could mean writing a letter to an ancestor and then ceremoniously burning or burying it or crafting a symbolic representation of what needs to be released and then letting it go. It's a personal ritual to say goodbye to the past and usher in the future. You may find these rituals very cathartic as you release the emotions, old stories, and energetic ties that have held you down.

- **Reconciliation Conversations:** Some wounds can be healed with conversation. These conversations are long overdue, and everyone knows it, but nobody is willing to take the first step. A family is built on close ties, and sometimes, reconnecting is the only way to heal the family. Your dad and your brother haven't spoken in years, and it could all be because of a misunderstanding. Conversations are important because everyone gets a chance to share their perspectives. During the conversation, their feelings are validated, their pain is honored, and forgiveness is possible for the first time in a long time. All some people need is a safe space to have difficult but necessary conversations, a space where they can be listened to. You may not believe it, but one conversation can heal an entire lineage.

- **Intergenerational Trauma Work:** The investigation you are currently performing on the emotional and psychological wounds in your lineage is a necessary step to breaking these traumatic cycles. Intergenerational trauma healing may include personal or family therapy, breathwork, somatic awareness, and inner child healing.

- **Energy Work:** Energy healing, chakra balancing, and ancestral lineage clearing are all ways to release the imprints and patterns that are stuck in your family's energetic field. Any kind of energy work can interact with the energies in your bloodline to clear blockages and restore balance.

- **Family Constellation Therapy:** This therapeutic approach is not as popular as it is effective. Its strategy is to expose the relationships, loyalties, and dynamics within your family system so you can better understand it. It brings your family tree to life and reveals everyone's emotional position in relation to other family members. There isn't a single therapeutic approach similar to this anywhere in the world. You get to see and interact with your family tree, and it is only when you see what is broken that you can understand how to fix it.
- **Journaling/Reflection:** At this point, you must have written so many things in your journal already. That little book and its contents will help you understand your family history, process your emotions, and have some much-needed conversation with yourself. Your journal is a physical record of your healing journey, and you can refer back to it as often as you need while you continue to grow and heal.
- **Meditations and Visualizations:** There have been a few guided meditations and visualization exercises so far, so this isn't news to you. They are such potent practices on their own and can be used for a myriad of things, but they are especially powerful when used to connect with your ancestral lineage. Your ancestors are there, waiting to guide you if only you take the time to listen. Meditation and visualizations are how you listen.

Integrate meditation exercises.[18]

Tips to Prepare for the Healing Journey

- Draw yourself a warm bath with Epsom salts or essential oils to release tension or negative energy.
- Do some light yoga or stretching to get your body moving and your energy flowing.
- Make yourself a cup of herbal tea to help calm your nerves.
- Spend some time in nature, even if it's sitting outside for only 10 minutes. Connect with the earth.
- Write down any feelings or intentions you have for your healing session. Get it out of your head and into your journal.
- Smudge your space with sage or palo santo to clear any stagnant or unwanted energies.
- Take deep, mindful breaths to center and ground yourself.
- Drink plenty of water to stay hydrated and support your body's natural healing processes.
- Don't eat heavy meals or anything too stimulating right before your healing.
- Dress comfortably in loose, breathable clothing that won't restrict your movement.
- Turn off your phone or silence the notifications.
- Remind yourself to approach this with an open mind and a compassionate heart. Trust the process.

Exercise 1: Hearing the Call

1. Go to a quiet, comfortable space where you can be alone for the next 15 to 20 minutes without any distractions. Your backyard patio works fine; your parked car with the windows rolled up is perfect – as long as it is safe and quiet.
2. Take some deep, centering breaths.
3. Silently ask yourself two powerful questions:
    - "What patterns in my life are asking to be healed?"
    - "What messages have I been receiving from my ancestors or my spirit?"

4. No overthinking; let your intuition guide you. What ancestral wound has come up lately that needs your attention? Are there unhealthy behaviors, beliefs, or relationship patterns that refuse to go away? What could your spirit be trying to tell you?
5. While you reflect on these questions, watch for any thoughts, emotions, or images that come to mind. Remember, any hits you get are exactly what you need to concentrate on.
6. What messages did you get? Write it down in your journal. Is there a specific message that stood out?
7. At the end of this exercise, write a short affirmation that symbolizes your intention for your healing journey. You could write:
    - "I embrace the journey of healing with courage, love, and grace."
    - "I am open to the wisdom and guidance of my ancestors and my spirit."
    - "I trust the process of my transformation and growth."
8. Hold on to this moment and trust that the answers you need will continue to reveal themselves at the right time. The call to heal is sacred, and you shouldn't rush it.
9. Take some deep breaths again, then open your eyes.

Exercise 2: Preparing for Healing

Smudging:
1. You'll need a smudge stick (a bundle of dried sage, sweetgrass, or palo santo), a fireproof container to hold the burning herbs, and a fan to help direct the smoke.
2. Hold the bundle and light the end. Gently blow on it until you see a steady flame. Then, blow it out so it's smoldering and forming smoke.
3. Waft the smoke over your body, concentrating on your head, heart, and hands. Imagine the smoke clearing the stagnant energies in your aura.
4. Mindfully move the smudge stick around the room so the smoke fills the air. Pay special attention to the corners and windowsills because bad energies tend to get stuck here.

5. While you cleanse, say your intention for the cleansing. Chant a mantra or say a prayer.
6. When you're done, squish the ember in your fireproof container. Use the fan to guide the last of the smoke out an open window or door.

Bath Ritual:
1. Assemble everything you'll need beforehand. You'll need bath salts, essential oils, candles, crystals, or anything else that calms you.
2. Light some candles, play music, and dim the lights.
3. Run the water to your preferred temperature, then add your bath salts, oils, or herbs.
4. Step into the tub and get comfortable. Breathe and let your muscles sink into the water.
5. Before fully submerging, set your intentions for why you're doing this ritual. What do you hope to release, restore, or invite in?
6. Now relax and let go. Quietly contemplate and open your mind to intuitive downloads.
7. If you're ready to start your healing journey, step out of the tub, drain it, and rinse off any residue. Pat your skin dry and go on to do your healing ritual.

Grounding:
1. Close your eyes if that helps you focus.
2. Imagine your energy flowing down through your body. Imagine this energy as roots growing from the base of your spine and into the earth below. In your mind's eye, see those roots extending deeper and deeper, anchoring you to the solid ground.
3. Breathe and feel your body weight sinking you down. Feel yourself becoming balanced and stable.
4. Imagine any excess nervous energy or tension draining out through the soles of your feet and being absorbed by the earth. Let it go.
5. You can also physically connect to the earth by standing barefoot on the grass or sitting on the ground.
6. Take as much time as you need to ground yourself before starting your healing.

Crystals for Ancestral Healing Work

- **Obsidian:** Obsidian is a protective and grounding stone that you can use to establish a strong foundation for your ancestral healing journey. Before any rituals or meditation, hold an obsidian crystal in your hands and imagine it drawing out all the negative energies from your body and energy field. This crystal will protect you before and during your healing.

Obsidian.[14]

- **Amethyst:** Amethyst is the crystal to use if you want to enhance your connection to your ancestral wisdom. Place an amethyst crystal on your third eye chakra and allow it to open your psychic senses and boost your intuition so you receive clearer messages and visions from your ancestors.

Amethyst.[15]

- **Citrine:** Citrine amplifies your personal power and creativity. When working to metabolize and transmute ancestral wounds, hold this crystal in your palms. Feel its warm energy flow through you to dissolve any shame, fear, or victimhood. Imagine its power as bright as the sun, blazing away old patterns and making space for new ones.

Citrine.[16]

- **Carnelian:** Carnelian can link you to the courage and strength of your ancestors. If you feel stuck or disconnected during your healing process, place a carnelian in your hands. Feel its energy infusing your root chakra, grounding you, and replenishing your strength. This is the crystal to keep with you whenever you need motivation.

Carnelian.[17]

Exercise 3: How to Set Up a Family Altar

1. Choose a spot in your home for your altar. Look around and see if there's a quiet, peaceful corner or a little table that would be perfect for this. It could be in your living room, your bedroom, or even a hallway. The most important thing is that it's a place that is calm and intentional, somewhere you can easily visit every day.
2. Collect items that hold personal significance for you and your family. This could include old family photos, heirlooms, or a small statue that reminds you of home. It doesn't hurt to add natural elements like candles, fresh flowers, gemstones, or crystals. Choose these items intentionally; each one should have a special meaning and memory attached to it.
3. Once you have your meaningful objects, you'll need to arrange them on your altar. Let your intuition guide this arrangement, and trust that you can't get it wrong.
4. Feel free to rearrange or add new items as the seasons change, as your needs change, or if you feel divinely guided. You might want to switch out the flowers with the changing months or add any new heirlooms that you find.
5. Use this altar for daily prayers, quiet meditation, and to communicate with your ancestors. See it as their space inside your space.
6. Now, light a candle and say a prayer.

Chapter Five: Releasing Rituals: The Path to Forgiveness

Release work is any intentional practice that involves consciously letting go of negative emotions, beliefs, or restrictive attachments. It is a process that requires you to actively acknowledge and process your feelings, not suppress or avoid them. The goal of release work is to free yourself from old burdens so that you can move forward with a lighter heart, clarity, and peace.

To release something means to let go of it – to stop clinging to it, resisting it, or allowing it to have any power over you. You can release a chronic vendetta against someone who has done you wrong but also release any fear or anxiety you have about an uncertain outcome.

Releasing and letting go work hand in hand.[18]

Releasing is not the same as forgiveness. The two are related but far from identical. Forgiveness is choosing to pardon someone for a perceived wrong and to let go of your desire to get revenge. Release work, on the other hand, concentrates more on your internal experience. You literally will be releasing the negative emotions, thoughts, and opinions that you've been carrying, whether you've forgiven the person or situation or not.

That said, release work and forgiveness complement one another nicely. If you're able to forgive someone who has hurt you, it becomes easier to release the pain, anger, and resentment you've been holding on to. On the other side, releasing anger makes it easier to extend forgiveness because you're no longer drowning in the intensity of those painful emotions.

Release work tends to happen in a particular sequence:

- **Acknowledgment:** You must acknowledge and validate your feelings without judging or trying to change them. You can do this by writing them down, talking to a friend or therapist, or just sitting with them in meditation.
- **Exploration:** After acknowledgment comes exploration, meaning you need to get to the roots of your emotions and opinions. What from the past are they connected to? What role have your thoughts and assumptions played in shaping them? What wounds do they represent?
- **Letting Go:** After exploration, you then start the actual process of letting go. This could be through visualization exercises, rituals, journaling, or actively redirecting your attention and energy away from the things you're releasing.
- **Integration:** You thought that was the end, didn't you? For your release work to be complete, you need to integrate the lessons and clarity you've gained and intentionally choose how you want to move forward. If you release your anger at your ex-partner, you can decide not to speak to them, or you can decide that it doesn't matter and say hi the next time you see them. It all depends on what you know is best for you.

Forgiveness doesn't always automatically result in release. Some deep, painful wounds take time to forgive, and there must be conscious effort before true release happens. Release doesn't always come from forgiveness, either. You may need to release yourself from unhealthy attachments, limiting beliefs, or negative thought patterns that have nothing to do with forgiving someone else. This release has to do with freeing yourself from internal blockages, not external ones.

For example, imagine you had a falling out with a close friend. Forgiving them for their part in this dispute can release the anger and resentment you've been carrying, but you may also need to release yourself from your attachment to the friendship itself. You'll be letting go of how it used to be and accepting the new reality between the two of you. This broader release allows you to move forward without being haunted by the loss of the friendship.

Another example is when you need to release yourself from self-limiting beliefs, like "I'm not good enough" or "I can't do it." This release is internal. You're setting yourself free from the binds you've placed on your own potential. The point is that forgiveness can lead to release, *but release doesn't always require forgiveness.*

Unresolved Emotions and the Cycle of Suffering

Unresolved anger is a flame that never extinguishes. Anger, in its purest form, is a natural and valid emotional response to a perceived injustice or wound, but when it is left to smolder, it turns into a raging fire that consumes people from within. Holding onto anger is exhausting. It puts you on a hamster wheel and commands you to run, to waste a tremendous amount of energy, but never actually go anywhere.

Within the family, unresolved anger quickly transforms into a corrosive resentment that poisons communication and corrupts the family bond. It is a slow-acting toxin. Simple conversations turn into minefields, with everyone walking a tightrope, afraid to say the wrong words or statements and set each other off. The result is a strained family dynamic where loved ones drift apart even as they struggle to find common ground.

Anger is not the only cause of this. Unresolved guilt and shame are just as corrosive within the family unit, especially if these emotions are the result of intergenerational trauma. It is a weight that no one knows how to lift, and so it's ignored. The whole family pretends as if it doesn't exist, passing from generation to generation, if possible, until it grows strong enough to bind the bloodline in a karmic tie.

What family members may not realize is that by holding onto this resentment and refusing to let it go, they are fueling karmic cycles. All that resentment accumulating throughout the years from pain and misunderstanding turns into shackles that continue to pull everyone back into the past, no matter how much they would like to live in the future. It pokes at the family wound, and like a physical wound, if it is not treated with care and compassion, it will become infected and continue to cause pain.

Forgiveness is the way out. It is the salve that can heal those wounds. For every day you hold onto resentment, you send out a signal to the universe that you're not ready to let go, and the universe, in turn, responds by keeping you stuck within those same patterns that you very clearly refuse to let go of. However, when you choose forgiveness, you send out a very different message – one that says, "I'm ready to move on, and I'm ready to create something new."

Forgiveness Is a Journey

Forgiveness is such a misunderstood concept. You may think holding onto your anger is the only way to find happiness and security. You convince yourself that by protecting yourself and keeping your love and joy at a distance, you can avoid being hurt again, but that's the lie anger tells you – a trap that ends up imprisoning you in your fear and pain.

Forgiveness is the bridge that will take you from recycled anger to inner peace and unconditional love. You will not be pretending like the pain never happened or brushing it aside; you will be setting it free and, in the process, setting yourself free. You are so much more than the wounds you carry, and forgiveness lets you finally see that.

A powerful act such as this doesn't happen overnight, in a single day, or even in a week, not for you and definitely not for your family. It's a journey that requires patience, self-reflection, and dedication to confronting the depths of your history and the history of those you love. True forgiveness not –just to those who have wronged you directly but to and on behalf of your entire family tree – can heal your bloodline down to its very roots. Your wounds are real, and they deserve to be seen and honored. Take all the time you need to grieve what has been lost, to mourn the injustices you and your loved ones have survived. Cry the tears that need to be cried, and rage if that is what you need, for it is only by reaching the depths of the wound that you can finally begin to let it go.

Myths About Forgiveness

Myth: Forgiveness Means Forgetting

The idea that forgiveness requires you to simply "forget" the pain or wrong you've experienced has to be the most popular myth about forgiveness. You don't need to erase the memory of what happened to prove that it is forgiven. Forgiveness is not amnesia, but remembering it can be very triggering for many people, so it must mean you still haven't forgiven, right? No. Even after you've forgiven someone, the memory of what they did stays for a while, and there's nothing wrong with that. The only thing that matters is that you've decided not to let that memory control you anymore. Healing from any wound takes time, let alone a deep emotional wound. There will be times when the memory resurfaces, and you feel that pain all over again, but that doesn't mean you haven't forgiven; it just means you're human. You don't need to force yourself to pretend it never happened, but you need to reach a place where you can remember it without it consuming you. Forgiveness sets you free; it doesn't set the memory free, and soon enough, the memory will lose its power all on its own.

Myth: Forgiveness Requires Reconciliation

Another misconception people have is that forgiveness means you have to make peace with the person who hurt you (or even try to rebuild a relationship with them), but that's only a myth, a manipulative one at that. Forgiveness is an inherently internal process. It is an inside job that does not hinge on the other person's willingness or ability to make amends. You can choose to forgive regardless of whether the aggressor acknowledges their actions, apologizes, or even remains in your life. If you grew up with distant or abusive parents, you can choose to forgive them, even if they never apologize or try to make amends. It will help you heal and move on. In this case, forgiveness is about reclaiming your power and worth, regardless of what your parents do. You don't have to wait for the other person to be ready or willing to reconcile. Your decision to forgive is you letting go of your need for their validation or approval. You are freeing yourself from the anger and bitterness to make space for a future that is not defined by the past. Yes, sometimes forgiveness can lead to reconciliation, but that is only a potential outcome, not the goal.

Myth: Forgiveness Is a Sign of Weakness

When thinking about forgiveness, it's easy to imagine it as a sign of weakness, like you're letting the person who hurt you off the hook or giving in to them, but forgiveness takes an incredible amount of strength and courage. If you experienced a betrayal or abuse, the decision to forgive doesn't mean you are weak. It takes so much strength to open your heart and choose compassion, even after going through unimaginable pain and suffering. Far from being weak, forgiveness projects strength and self-love. Every time you forgive, you reach into the depths of your humanity, your capacity for empathy, and your ability to alchemize your pain into something positive. You're not giving in or giving up; you're taking back control and affirming your worth despite the most devastating circumstances.

Barriers to Forgiveness

Fear of Losing Power or Control

Getting hurt often feels like you've lost control of the situation, so holding onto anger and resentment can make you feel like you still have some power over what happened. Forgiving the person who hurt you definitely feels like giving up that power. It's normal to worry that if you let go of your anger, the other person will get away with it or that you'll lose your leverage. It's scary to think about making yourself vulnerable again, but you won't be making yourself vulnerable because forgiveness is about you and you alone. You're not letting them go; you're letting it go.

Feeling That Forgiving Minimizes the Harm Done

Some people have been cut so deep that they really believe forgiving the person who did it is the same as saying, "It wasn't that bad." They worry that forgiving will make the other person think their actions were acceptable, and that worry is valid because there are manipulative people who will absolutely see forgiveness as a free pass. As far as they are concerned, if it was that bad, you wouldn't forgive them, but they can't fathom how wrong they are. Forgiveness doesn't guarantee a clean slate. It isn't absolution, neither does it mean the pain wasn't a big deal. You can choose to forgive and find peace without reconciliation.

Deep Emotional Pain or Unresolved Trauma

Forgiveness is extremely difficult when the wound is still raw and painful. Soul-crushing wounds leave lasting scars, and the thought of letting go of that pain can feel impossible. You're afraid that if you forgive, you'll forget and not honor your suffering, but there's nothing to fear. True forgiveness triggers the integration of your pain into your story without letting it define you. It frees you from being a victim and gives you your life back. None of this means you have to rush into forgiveness, but when you do forgive, it'll only be for your sake.

Feeling That Self-Forgiveness Is Not Relevant or Can Be Bypassed

As hard as it is to forgive others, it is so much easier to do that than to forgive yourself. Why do you think your mistakes are unforgivable? Why do you treat yourself like you don't deserve the same compassion you extend to others? You're human, and every human makes mistakes. No one is perfect, no matter how much they wish they could be. Give yourself grace and compassion in the same capacity you give everyone else. Self-forgiveness is not the same thing as lacking accountability. To even forgive in the first place, you must acknowledge what you have done and then give yourself the grace to grow and do better. Your mistakes won't define you.

Exercise 1: Journaling Prompts for Forgiveness

Any time you need to forgive someone, whether it is difficult or not, it could be of great help to sort through your thoughts and emotions first. Journaling might give you clarity, release, and a path forward when the road to forgiveness feels long and difficult.

You can do this with any of these prompts:

- What are the specifics of the situation or person that you are struggling to forgive? Describe in your own words what happened and how you felt about the situation.
- What was the biggest betrayal you experienced in this situation? How has that affected you and your life?
- When you think about this person/situation, what strong emotions arise from within you? Is it anger, sadness, shame, or fear? Describe the feeling.
- In what ways has holding onto this pain or resentment affected your daily life, your relationships, and your health? Be honest about the costs.

- If you were able to completely forgive, what do you imagine it would feel like in your heart and body?
- Is there anything positive you might be able to take from this painful situation if you chose forgiveness? Could it help you grow in some way?
- How might your life change if you were able to let go of your anger and forgive? What would be different or better?
- What worst-case scenario do you fear might happen if you forgave this person? How realistic is that fear, really?
- If you could say anything to the person who hurt you, what would you say?
- Try to imagine yourself in the other person's shoes. What reason or motivation might they have had for them to perform this deed? Can you find any empathy or understanding?
- Think of a time in your life when you've hurt or wronged someone. How did it feel to be forgiven by them?
- Who in your life has modeled forgiveness, and what can you learn from their example?
- What does "letting go" mean to you, and how might it apply to this situation you're working on?
- What is your intuition telling you about forgiving this person, even if it feels difficult right now?
- If you could give advice to someone else going through this, what would you say?
- What small steps could you take today towards forgiveness?
- What does true forgiveness look like to you?

Exercise 2: Releasing Through Ritual

You will be casting a protection circle around your family altar for this ritual, and while you may not even need it, you are performing a release ritual and attempting to connect with your ancestors who exist in the unseen realm along with other entities who may or may not be drawn to the negative emotions you are about to release. All of this is to make the process as safe and as comfortable as possible.

1. For the circle, you'll need a representation of the four elements. A candle for fire, a crystal for earth, a bowl of water, and incense for air.
2. Smudge your space with palo santo.
3. Place the elements in the four cardinal directions around the altar. Earth in the north, fire in the south, air in the east, and water in the west.
4. Step inside the space and imagine a glowing, protective light expanding outward from your body until it touches the elements.
5. Call upon your ancestors and any of your spirit guides to bless and strengthen the circle.
6. Take out a piece of paper and a pen. Write a letter to the ancestor you need to forgive (You can do this for a living person as well). Don't hold anything back; pour out all of your feelings and write until you have nothing left to say.
7. When you are finished, re-read your letter and validate the emotions you have expressed. Then, carefully fold the paper and place it in the center of your altar.
8. Look at the letter for however long you want and validate the pain and difficulty in this situation.
9. When you feel ready, light the letter on fire in a fireproof container or ashtray. As you watch the paper burn, say out loud, "This pain is released to the universe. I choose the path of forgiveness and freedom."

    (**Safety disclaimer:** *Be extremely careful when burning anything, and always have a fire extinguisher nearby. Never leave a burning letter unattended*).
10. When you are finished, take a few deep breaths and step out of the circle.
11. To dismantle the circle, remove the elements in the order you placed them.

Exercise 3: Ho'oponopono

Ho'oponopono is an ancient Hawaiian practice that teaches how the inner world and outer world are connected and that everything you think, feel, and do affects not just yourself but the whole world. Imagine for a second that your mind is a garden. If left unattended, it will get overgrown with weeds that spread out in all directions. Ho'oponopono is a way to tend to this garden, clear out the weeds, and make space for new, healthy growth.

Ho'oponopono is a way of life that simplifies letting go.[19]

Hawaiians believe in taking 100% responsibility for your life. This means recognizing that everything you experience, good or bad, is a reflection of what's happening inside of you, and this is not to blame you but to show you that you have the power to make changes. Ho'oponopono teaches that the true self, your divine essence, is buried under all the debris in your mind, and if you can clear out those old memories and beliefs, you can reconnect with your authentic self. Modern Ho'oponopono uses the phrases "I'm sorry," "Please forgive me," "Thank you," and "I love you" to do this inner work.

By saying "I'm sorry," you're taking responsibility for the negative thoughts, feelings, or actions that have contributed to the problems in your life. It's an apology to yourself and a humble acceptance that you're not perfect, and there's nothing wrong with that.

When you say, "Please forgive me," it is a heartfelt plea to the universe, your higher self, and anyone you may have hurt. It's a request to be released from the past – the guilt, the shame, the resentment. This plea for forgiveness isn't just mending relationships with others; it also repairs your relationship with yourself.

In Ho'oponopono, saying "Thank you" is so much more than just good manners. It's a declaration of trust – an acknowledgment that the healing process has already begun, even if you can't see the full results yet. When you express gratitude, you're aligning your heart with abundance and possibility. You're saying, "I believe in this journey, and I'm grateful for every step."

Finally, you say, "I love you." These 3 words are the beating heart of Ho'oponopono. By saying, "I love you," you're reconnecting with the divine essence within yourself. You're declaring your self-acceptance and compassionately embracing all of you. But this is more than self-love; when you say, "I love you," you're dissolving the barriers between yourself and the world around you.

The order in which you say these phrases is not as important as your sincerity and intention. Some would say there's a natural progression to the phrases. They start with "I'm sorry" to acknowledge the issue or problem that needs attention. Then they move to "Please forgive me" to let go and make space for healing. Next, they say "Thank you" to express gratitude for the transformation that's already happening, and finally, they arrive at "I love you" to reconnect them to divine love and unity.

That is one way to do it, but there's really no formula to this. Some people prefer to begin with "I love you" because they want to establish a connection to their divinity first. Others would rather start with gratitude for the opportunity to heal in the first place. Let your heart guide your process. Your sincerity and intention are all that matter. When you are finished, write down any downloads or thoughts you had during your session.

Exercise 4: Two-Chair Gestalt Therapy

For this exercise, you will be role-playing as yourself and the person you are trying to forgive. The idea is to step into their shoes and see the situation from their perspective. This can lead to more understanding and empathy, even for someone who has hurt you.

Step 1: Sit in a chair or on the floor and breathe to relax.

Step 2: Close your eyes and imagine the person you're trying to forgive sitting across from you. Picture them clearly in your mind – what do they look like? How are they sitting or moving? What emotions do you feel as you see them in your mind's eye?

Step 3: Speak out loud and share your honest feelings with this person. Tell them how their actions have made you feel, what you've been struggling with, and anything else you need to say. Speak from your heart.

Step 4: Now, switch roles. Imagine yourself as the other person, sitting across from yourself. Try to get into their head. What do you think they might be feeling or experiencing? What pain could they be dealing with?

Step 5: Respond to yourself, speaking as the other person now. Try to explain their point of view, their reasons, and their motivations. Don't judge or defend; just try to understand where they're coming from.

Step 6: Continue switching roles, going back and forth between your perspective and theirs. With each switch, go deeper into the other person's experience. Ask yourself questions like:

- What wounds or issues might be driving their behavior?
- How can I have more compassion for what they're going through?
- How can I start to see their humanity, even if I don't agree with their actions?

Step 7: See if you can reach a place of mutual understanding and forgiveness. Don't force it, but be open to the possibility of letting go of your anger.

Exercise 5: Affirmations for Self-Forgiveness

- I forgive myself for my mistakes. I am only human.
- I release any guilt or shame that I've been holding on to.
- I accept that I am not perfect, and that's okay.
- I am worthy of forgiveness, just as I am.
- I am learning and growing, even through my imperfections.
- I release the need to be flawless. Perfection is an impossible standard.
- I replace self-criticism with self-compassion.
- I forgive myself for not always meeting my own expectations.
- I am deserving of love, even when I make mistakes.
- I am worthy of healing and inner peace, flaws and all.
- I celebrate my willingness to forgive and improve.
- I am enough, just as I am in this moment.
- I forgive myself for the mistakes I have made.

Exercise 6: Advanced Self-Healing and Releasing Ritual

1. Find a quiet space and cast a protective circle like in exercise 2.
2. Get into a relaxed, meditative state and center yourself with a few deep breaths.
3. Think about a repetitive emotion or pattern you've noticed in your life – maybe it's your guilt, fear, self-doubt, or something else. Imagine this emotion as a tangible object inside your body. It could be a knot in your stomach, a heavy stone on your chest, or a dark cloud in your mind.
4. Gently place your hands over your heart and close your eyes. Connect with that emotional object within you. Ask it, "What are you here to teach me?"
5. Open your mind and listen. What thoughts, memories, or sensations are coming to you? Feel whatever comes up, and don't judge it.

6. Sit with this emotion and imagine the object gradually dissolving into light. See it releasing its grip on you and floating away.
7. When you're ready, take a deep breath and say out loud, "I release what no longer serves me. I embrace healing and wholeness."
8. Trust that with each emotion you release, you're becoming more whole, more free.

Chapter Six: Breaking the Chains: Healing Generational Patterns

It is impossible to exist in isolation. As humans, we depend on each other for our most basic needs, such as food, shelter, and healthcare. We learn from each other and find meaning and purpose through our connections. From the day you're born, you have a community – your family. It is the first and most important community you belong to. They're with you from the very beginning. They feed you, keep you safe, and teach you the basic skills and values that define who you become.

Break the chains to start a new cycle in your life.[30]

Family is the source of your earliest and most formative memories. Within the family, you learn how to communicate, solve problems, and build relationships. The bonds you form with your parents, siblings, and other family members are hardwired into your psyche and continue to influence you for the rest of your life. They feel essential to your identity and your place in the world. Even if your family isn't the healthiest or most functional, there's usually an almost automatic loyalty and attachment that forms. That family is your whole world when you're young, and the prospect of separating from it is terrifying.

Anyone would be afraid to lose that support system. What if you speak up about the problems in your family, and they reject you? What if you try to set boundaries and end up all alone? Those consequences can feel catastrophic, so it's easier to go along with the status quo, even if it's obviously dysfunctional.

On top of that, shame and guilt could also be wrapped up in it. You may feel embarrassed by your family's issues or worry that you're betraying them by not being able to keep things together. That responsibility and loyalty you feel can seem almost unbreakable. All of this creates a psychological and emotional trap. You see that the dynamics in your family are unhealthy, but your loyalty and attachment make it exceptionally hard to step away. It feels safer, in a twisted way, to keep participating in those behaviors because the alternative is scary and uncertain.

Generally, people aren't entirely conscious of how much family loyalty is propelling their choices. It operates on a gut level - an automatic pull to preserve the family unit, no matter what.

Growing up in certain family dynamics can desensitize you to certain things. The most abnormal actions feel completely normal. If yelling, drinking problems, or controlling behavior has been in your family your whole life, you may not even recognize it as dysfunctional behavior. It's just how things are. It's like that saying, "The fish doesn't know it's in water." When you're submerged in something your whole life, it becomes invisible to you - natural, unavoidable. It's not until you step outside that family system or experience something different that the fog clears. Behaviors that felt acceptable or even inevitable finally look as problematic as they are. Finally, you're aware.

Healing Begins with Awareness

One way to think about awareness is to imagine a spotlight. Complete awareness means the spotlight is shining brightly, illuminating everything in your immediate environment, including your mental workings. However, sometimes, the spotlight can dim or shift, and your awareness becomes limited or focused on one particular aspect of your experience. While you read this, your awareness might narrow down to the words on the page, and whether you know this or not, you probably temporarily tuned out the sounds and sights around you. That's your awareness spotlight getting a little smaller and more concentrated. Everyone does this to some degree; our attention naturally drifts in and out, focusing on one thing at a time.

With family, sometimes you see only what you want to see. You unconsciously focus only on things that are comfortable or familiar, and so you ignore the regular angry outbursts, the addictive behaviors, and the quiet put-downs because confronting them would be too hard. It's a defense mechanism. In its attempts to protect you from pain, your brain filters out the parts of reality that are too threatening. If you were to truly see all the dysfunction in your family, it might shatter the image you've built up in your head. Your parents or siblings might not seem so loving or supportive anymore, and so you make excuses for those bad behaviors or convince yourself that "it's not that bad." You become an expert at pretending everything is fine. Anything to avoid rocking the boat, anything to preserve your family as a safe haven.

Unfortunately, selective awareness does more harm than good. Your refusal to see the reality of your family's dysfunction makes it that much harder to bring about necessary change. This dysfunction only gets worse, generation after generation. But it doesn't have to be, not when you can do something about it.

Exercise 1: Family System Mapping

1. Get your journal. Draw your family tree with as many family members as you can remember. Include your parents, grandparents, siblings, aunties, uncles, and cousins. It's okay if you don't know or can't remember every single name or detail. Write what you know.
2. When you write each name, what feelings do you get about that person? Some names might bring warm, good feelings, while others could come with unpleasant emotions. Make a note next to their name on the tree about the feeling you get from their energy. For example, when you write your grandmother's name, you may feel upset and protective, but your uncle's name makes you feel on edge. Combine your intuition with what you know about them to get this as accurately as possible.
3. After you've mapped out your whole family, look at the map. What do you notice? Are there branches that feel lighter and more positive versus parts that feel heavier or off-balance?
4. It is possible that the women in your family mostly have fierce yet nurturing energy, and the men are quiet and emotionally distant. Or there could be that one ancestor who seems to have had a big influence on the entire family, for better or worse.
5. While you observe, use different colored pens or highlighters to mark the areas that feel more or less unbalanced or difficult. These are the parts of your family tree that could use extra attention when it comes to the healing process.
6. The next thing to do is ask yourself some questions like:
   o Who in my family seems to have the most positive, light-filled energy? How can I connect with that more?
   o Where do I feel the most pain or trauma in my family's history? What can I do to help heal those wounds?
   o Are there any unhealthy patterns that always carry over into the next generation? How can I break that cycle?

After you reflect on these questions, set some intentions for how you want to move forward. You may decide to make peace with a sibling or be more proud of your ancestors. Or just have more compassion for the things your family has been through. This exercise isn't to judge or nitpick your family but to identify the areas that need healing the most.

Exercise 2: Guided Ancestral Meditation

1. Sit down or lie down comfortably.
2. Inhale, hold for three seconds and then exhale. Do this three times to center yourself.
3. Close your eyes and imagine that you're standing at the base of an old, large tree. This tree will represent your family lineage, and each branch represents an ancestor. Feel your connection to this tree because you are intimately connected to it.
4. Look at the tall, strong tree trunk anchored firmly into the earth. Reach out and place your hand on the tree. Feel how solid it is - how alive. Remove your hand and sit at the base of the tree.
5. Look around, and you should notice that a bright energy field surrounds the tree. This is all your ancestors' collective wisdom, life force, and unconditional love. Feel their presence; let it surround you.
6. Can you describe what it feels like to you when you feel this ancestral energy? Is it soothing and reassuring? Or is it unsettling? Whatever you feel, don't judge it; just observe.
7. It's time to concentrate on any issues or questions that have been on your mind lately. These could be behaviors or thoughts that you'd like to shift, relationships that need tending, or life decisions you're trying to make. Silently ask your ancestors for guidance and support as you do this.
8. Touch the tree again and imagine an energy surge flowing through you. Hold that energy and wait to see if you get visions, memories, or clarity.
9. These are messages from your ancestors, and you should allow them to unfold naturally. Trust that the messages you get are for a reason, even if you can't decode them just yet.
10. Thank your ancestors for their presence and wisdom.
11. Inhale deeply, then exhale.
12. Open your eyes.

Exercise 3: Affirmation Journaling

Affirmations work because they override the human natural tendency to see only problems and weaknesses. Intentionally directing your attention to what you want to achieve shows you a world filled with possibility, not limitation, and doing this every day trains your mind to find solutions and make the best of every situation.

Affirmation journaling is very suggestive of a positive mindset.[81]

1. Get your journal and pen.
2. Inhale and exhale to center yourself, then think about a particular belief or theme that's been present in your family for as long as you can remember. A belief that even you internalized. In your family, maybe most of you suffer self-doubt and insecurity, or you have a habit of always putting others first. Or a voice in your head telling you that you're not good enough or don't deserve happiness.
3. In your journal, write down this negative pattern in as much detail as you can. For example: "In my family, we've always believed that we're unlucky and that good things don't happen to us." Or "My family functions from a scarcity mindset, always afraid of not having enough."
4. Describe this pattern and watch how it makes you feel. Does it frustrate you? Are you sad? Ashamed? Or resigned because "that's just the way it is"? Write down these thoughts and feelings as they come.

5. Think about how this pattern has shown up in your life. Where have you seen it play out? Your relationships? Your work? Your self-image? How has it held you back from being yourself?

6. Now, we need to reframe this negative pattern into a positive affirmation. This is your chance to create a new reality to replace the old, limiting cycle. For example, if the pattern was "We're always unlucky," you could replace it with, "I create my own luck and attract abundance into my life." Or if the pattern was "My family is afraid of not having enough," you could say, "My family and I are financially secure, and I trust that all our needs are provided for."

7. Write this new affirmation in your journal and take a minute to feel its energy. What do you think it would be like to embody this belief? How would it change your thoughts, your behaviors, and your whole outlook on life?

8. Whenever the old, familiar pattern resurfaces, go back to your journal and reread your affirmation.

Exercise 4: Cord Cutting Ritual

1. Meditate on what you'd like to release from your life. This could be a relationship, past trauma, or any emotional attachment that has been draining you. Get clear on what you want to let go of and what kind of positive energy you'd like to invite within yourself instead.

2. Write down your intentions on a piece of paper or in your journal. This will be your focal point during the ritual.

3. Choose an area for your ritual. If your family altar is set up, it'll be perfect for this.

4. Cleanse the area with palo santo or cedar.

5. Breathe and be present in your body. Feel your feet firmly planted on the ground and let any anxious or scattered energy flow down into the earth.

6. Close your eyes and bring your awareness to your heart center. Imagine a cord with one end connected to your heart and the other connecting you to the person, situation, or emotion you want to release. Emotions like anger, pain, jealousy, etc., may try to distract you, but don't let them in. Remain neutral.

7. Imagine the cord fraying and detaching from your heart. When this happens, say, "I am completely and fully released from you."
8. Feel the cord disintegrate into healing light.
9. You can reinforce your intentions by repeating affirmations:
    - "I'm letting go of this connection with love and appreciation for what it taught me."
    - "I'm not defined by my past anymore. I'm free to write my own story."
    - "I'm whole and complete just as I am."
    - "The universe is rearranging things for me, and I welcome this transition with open arms."

Exercise 5: Rewriting the Narrative

Your family doesn't have to recycle the same old negative stories that may have defined the past but don't have to define the future. You can rewrite the narrative and seal your intergenerational wounds. You can heal the bloodline one narrative at a time.

Old Negative Narrative	New Positive Narrative
"My family has always been unlucky."	"My family is strong, and we are attracting abundance and prosperity."
"The women in my family are always expected to take care of everyone else."	"The women in my family are powerful, nurturing leaders who are learning to honor their own needs alongside the needs of others."
"No one in my family ever achieved their dreams."	"My family is full of talented, ambitious people who boldly chase their dreams and make them a reality."

Old Negative Narrative	New Positive Narrative
"My family can't be trusted. You have to look out for yourself."	"My family is not perfect, but we are a supportive, loving community that looks out for one another. We can depend on each other."
"The men in my family are weak and unreliable."	"The men in my family are strong, responsible, and caring."
"We'll always struggle to make ends meet."	"My family is financially abundant and secure. We have everything we need and more."
"No one in my family is ever really happy."	"Happiness and joy come naturally to my family."
"The older generation always knows better than the younger ones."	"There is wisdom in every generation. We learn from one another."
"My family is destined to repeat the same mistakes over and over."	"Every generation in my family learns from the past. We have broken free."
"No one in my family ever takes accountability for their actions."	"My family members are accountable, self-aware, and committed to personal growth."
"My lineage isn't anything to be proud of."	"I am proud of my family."

Exercise 6: Ancestor Healing and Cleansing Micro-Rituals

For this exercise, you'll be performing elemental cleansing and healing rituals, but on a very small scale. They are called micro-rituals, not because they are not as potent but because of their simplicity and size.

Fire Ritual:

1. You'll need a pen and some paper. As always, take as many deep breaths as you need to center yourself.
2. On your paper, write down any negative patterns, limiting beliefs, or ancestral traumas that you're ready to release. Be as specific as you can. There could be an addiction problem in your family or an unhealthy codependent dynamic between the women and their partners. Or perhaps you want to finally release the belief that you'll never be good enough. Write it down.
3. After writing it all down on paper, it's time to let it go. Get a fireproof container and carefully light the paper on fire. As you watch the paper curl and disintegrate, imagine all of that heavy, stuck energy being burned away. Say, "I release this pattern. I am free."
4. Breathe and feel the relief that comes with letting the baggage go. The paper may be gone, but the healing has only just begun.

Water Ritual

1. You'll need a bowl or container filled with clean, fresh water.
2. Sit in a quiet room alone and hold the bowl in your hands.
3. Gaze into the water and think about the generational traumas and imprints that have traveled down your family tree to the present generations. Imagine all of that negative energy flowing into the water. Imagine it being absorbed and purified.
4. Speak out loud, "I cleanse this energy from my family tree. I am creating a new future for my lineage."
5. Then, for the release, slowly pour the water outside and watch it soak into the earth. Imagine the water carrying away all your ancestral baggage, leaving behind a clean, fresh foundation for you to build upon.

Earth Ritual

This final micro-ritual involves planting a tree – a living, growing symbol of your commitment to the healing process and the positive change happening in your family.

1. Choose a tree that represents the type of energy and transformation you're hoping for. For example, an oak tree could mean strength, stability, and wisdom. A fruit tree can signify abundance, nourishment, and new growth. Or a flowering tree could mean joy, beauty, and bright new beginnings.
2. Dig a hole and place the seed in the earth. As you do this, meditate on your family's history and the patterns you're ready to release. Speak your intentions out loud. Say, "With the planting of this tree, I am honoring the wisdom of my ancestors and making a commitment to build a new legacy for my family."
3. Plant this tree somewhere nearby so you can visit and tend it.

These micro-rituals are not required for perfecting or complicating the healing process. Their power comes from your sincere intention and the consciousness you bring to the process. The power comes from you; the elements are simply a conduit for that power.

Exercise 7: Advanced Journey to Heal the Ancestral Line

1. Go to your family altar and sit peacefully for a few minutes. Cleanse the area with sage.
2. Take a few deep breaths to settle in, and while you settle, think about why this ancestral healing journey is important to you. Are there things about your family you'd like to understand? Or do you already understand them, and all that's left is transformation? Set your intention for this exercise and say it out loud. An example is, "I'm here to connect with my ancestors and heal the wounds and imbalances in my family lineage."
3. Imagine roots growing from under your feet, extending down into the earth. Feel the solid, grounding support of the Earth mother. She's here to hold and sustain you as you go on this journey.
4. See a path appear in front of you. This path leads to a doorway or portal. This is the threshold to the ancestral realm.

5. Inhale deeply, then exhale.
6. Step through the doorway, trusting that you are safe and guided by forces you can not see.
7. When you enter this sacred space, call upon a spirit guide, an animal guide, or an ancestor who is already healed and willing to assist you.
8. In your mind's eye, see a long line of your ancestors stretching out before you - the most recent generations are closest, and the ancient ones are farther in the distance. Can you feel their presence?
9. If you can, go on to examine their energy. Who seems burdened or troubled? Who appears at peace? Let the impressions, emotions, or images come to you on their own.
10. If you sense any inherited pain or trauma, ask your guide to point you to its source. You may be shown a specific ancestor, a moment in time, or a symbolic representation of the wound.
11. Now imagine a warm light radiating from your heart center. Gently direct this light toward the ancestor or symbol that represents the wound. Watch this light dissolve the pain, anger, and fear and replace it with love, peace, and forgiveness. Feel lightness and relief spread through your body as this healing process takes place.
12. Open your mind to receiving wisdom from your ancestors. They may communicate with you through words, images, or feelings. Feel their guidance and healing energy flow through you. Let it wash over your mind, body, and spirit.
13. Before you leave, say thank you to your ancestors and your spirit guide for their help. Send loving energy to your entire lineage.
14. Take some deep breaths, step back through the doorway, and return to the present moment.

Chapter Seven: Honoring the Ancestors: Rebuilding Bonds and Reclaiming Power

All your ancestors were once living people. They had hopes, dreams, and a story of their own. Your great-grandparents were once teenagers with ambition and possibilities. They grew up, crossed paths, and fell in love. Soon after, they got married and started a family. Your grandparents were likely born into that family and had their own experiences growing up. They had favorite childhood memories, hobbies they enjoyed, or moments in their life that they will never forget. When they became adults, they, too, made choices that affected the direction of the family tree.

There's a balance between honoring your ancestors and reclaiming your power.[22]

Your parents, too, whom you know so well, were once young people maneuvering the world, finding their way, and preparing to welcome you into their lives. The decisions they made, from their careers to their relationships, all led to the moment you were born. When you really think about it, every single one of your ancestors, going back many generations, was a real person who laughed, loved, struggled, and persevered. Their lives, as ordinary or extraordinary as they may have been, all contributed to bringing you into existence.

Looking in the mirror right now, you'll see physical proof of this ancestral legacy. The features you inherited, the mannerisms you've adopted, and the talents you were born with were determined to a large extent by your bloodline. How you move and carry yourself, the cadence of your speech, not to mention some of your instinctive reactions – these behaviors were either learned or inherited. You could share a nervous habit with your grandmother or have the exact laugh as your great-uncle. You are not just one person but the culmination of many who still live on within you.

This is why your life must mirror the respect and honor you should have for your lineage. You have been entrusted to continue the story – a responsibility that should not be taken lightly. Their sacrifices and successes make it clear that you have a duty to live a life worthy of their legacy. Your great-grandparents may have fought for their freedom, going through heaven-knows-what to ensure a better future for their descendants. The least you can do is make the most of the opportunities they fought so hard to give you.

For all their strengths, they weren't perfect. It's fair to want to gloss over the more difficult chapters of your family's past. It's fair to want to focus only on the positives. It's fair if you want to believe that your ancestors led charmed lives, never suffered, and did nothing wrong. It's fair, but only to you, not to them. It is not the truth, and it is most definitely not their truth. No one makes it through life unscathed. One of your grandparents may have suffered from addiction or been an abuser. Your great-grandparents may have been poor, discriminated against, or lived through unspeakable trauma. The darker moments in your family's story are just as much a part of their legacy as the good parts. Your ancestors were heroes, flawless heroes. They were real people who did real things, some of which still affect the family tree today – things that need to be uprooted and healed.

Your ancestors are counting on you to carry the torch forward to greater success. They are hoping you heal the bloodline in ways they didn't or couldn't. They may not have done everything right, but you can do justice to their memory. You are on this healing journey to become the best of what your lineage has to offer, and in doing so, you'll be honoring their memory and creating a promising future for your bloodline.

Benefits of Connecting with Your Ancestors

Access to Their Strengths and Talents

A connection with your ancestors is a connection to their strengths, talents, and skills. Learning about their lives, you could discover gifts that you probably even inherited. You could have the same green thumb as your great-grandfather or the same musical ear as your grandmother. These talents aren't a coincidence; they're your genetic inheritance, waiting to be understood, activated, and developed. And it's not just skills; an ancestral connection also means access to the strength, determination, and strong work ethic that have defined your ancestors. Their toughness, grit, and drive are all there inside you, regardless of whether you are aware of it or not. Their legacy has become yours, and they wouldn't have it any other way.

Similarities Between Your Stories and Theirs

As you learn more about your ancestors' lives, you might be surprised by how much your experiences actually parallel theirs. The exact details could be different, but you'll find the same core emotions and struggles in multiple generations. Your great-grandmother's loneliness could look a lot like the isolation you've gone through. Your grandfather's fierce drive to provide for his family sounds more or less like how you feel. Connections like these collapse the distance between time and culture, and you finally understand that your ancestors aren't distant, unfamiliar figures; they're kin. They've been through similar joys and pains as you. Their stories are your stories, and they used to be human, too.

A Deeper Connection to Your Heritage

When you make an effort to understand your ancestors' lived realities, you're automatically more connected to your cultural heritage. The understanding here does not concern the surface-level information, like the foods, the festivals, or the family heirlooms. It's a little deeper into the hard-won wisdom and traditions that have sustained your people for generations. This understanding might give you a new appreciation for the sacrifices your ancestors have made or more respect for a tradition that has been in your family for centuries. This heightened cultural awareness connects the past to the present as you finally understand the multigenerational story that is your bloodline.

Clarity on Unresolved Issues in the Present

One of the most powerful gifts from connecting with your ancestry is the clarity it brings to problems and unhealthy patterns that have been left to fester in the bloodline - patterns that are playing out in your life right now. Some of your problems have roots buried so deep in your ancestors' stories that you'll never discover them unless you dig to find them. You may have inherited codependent tendencies from your grandfather, who was also codependent in his love life. There may be traces of your great-uncle's anger issues within your brother. The answers are sometimes hidden in the past, and this knowledge is the first step toward real healing. You're not just a person battling your demons; you're a link in a chain, and the demons may not even be yours.

Guidance and Protection on Your Healing Journey

Ancestors will always protect their own. You're not alone. Your ancestors stand with you. Their energy and essence are still powerfully felt and accessible. When there is uncertainty in your life, a connection to your ancestors opens a channel through which you receive intuitive downloads, dreams, or a feeling that they are with you, ever watchful. They can give you their wisdom, encouragement, and the strength to push forward in the areas they may have failed. They've been here, in these situations, before you; they have done all the human things, and they're eager to share the hard-won lessons they've learned, to be the guides walking alongside you, especially if you choose to collaborate with their energies, while you work to heal the family.

Access to Deep Collective Healing

When you shed the superficial layers to reveal the full truth about your family's past, you also reveal an opening for healing. The old traumas that have lived in the family for generations can finally be seen and released. The negative patterns and limiting beliefs that have taken root in your psyche, and that of every other family member, can also be identified and healed. Fractured relationships within your family can finally heal through the understanding and empathy you have made available to everyone. With an active ancestral connection, you become the bridge that helps reconnect the broken pieces and restore wholeness to your entire lineage. You are the conduit through which your family line will heal, and the entire collective is restored.

A Feeling of Belonging and Pride

This has to be the most powerful and life-affirming benefit of an active relationship with your ancestors. You are part of something larger than yourself, and this connection will only reassure you of that. You are not alone; you've never been. You stand on the shoulders of the people who have come before you, and you are connected to them. Yes, you inherited their trauma, but you also inherited all the beautiful parts, all the strong parts. Their successes are your successes. Their joys are your own, too. Their hopes and dreams are also yours. You will have nothing but empathy and pride for your origins. You'll understand that when you honor your ancestors, you are indirectly honoring yourself. You are bound to them as much as they are bound to you. You are their legacy.

Exercise 1: Ancestral Storytelling

Storytelling has been a staple in human history for as long as anyone can remember. It is how we connect with one another, teach each other, and, most importantly, understand the past. Storytelling is how you understand your family's past.

1. Think about which older family members you'd like to interview. This could be grandparents, grand-aunts or uncles, or family friends with interesting stories. Confirm that they're willing and have some time to chat.
2. Meditate on what you want to learn from these interviews. Do you want to hear about a particular topic, like their love stories? Or do you want to know where some family traditions originated? A focal point will guide your questions and make the conversation more interesting.
3. Pick a comfortable place for your interview. The more relaxing it is, the better.
4. Write down questions that encourage these family members to share the stories you want to hear. Take these, for example:
    - What was your childhood like? What are some of your favorite memories?
    - Was it hard growing up? How?

- Can you tell me about a time in your life that changed you forever?
- What family traditions have we forgotten?

5. You should use follow-up questions to make them go into greater detail, like:
   - How did that make you feel?
   - What did you learn from that?
   - What did you do after?
6. While you interview, listen closely. Show that you're interested. Nod and make eye contact. Don't cut them off; let them finish their thoughts.
7. Decide if you want to take notes or record the conversation. If you'd rather record, make sure you have their permission. Taking notes helps you concentrate, while recordings retain every detail for later.
8. Let the conversation flow. If they seem excited about something, let them continue. The best stories are the ones people actually want to tell.
9. After the interviews, think about organizing the stories into themes. You can group them by difficulty level, successes, or major life changes. This will show you where the patterns are in your family's history.
10. The next time you go through the stories, meditate on questions like:
    - What common problems did they all have to endure?
    - How did their choices influence the values in the family?
    - What lessons can I learn from their stories?
11. You can document all of this, turn it into an anthology, and share it with the family. You can also create a family scrapbook, a digital copy, or a special website to save these stories for future generations. Your heritage deserves to be celebrated, and this is one way to keep the memories alive.

Exercise 2: Ritual to Honor the Ancestors

1. This ritual is best done at your family altar and at a time when you won't be disturbed.
2. Before setting up, cleanse the space. If there's a window, open it for fresh air. Light some sage, or depending on how high your vibration is, you can imagine a clear, bright light engulfing the area.
3. On your altar, you should already have items that remind you of your ancestors. Add candles to that. You can use different colored candles depending on the energy you are aiming for. White candles, for example, are great for clarity. Blue candles are good for healing and communication (throat chakra).
4. Make this space very welcoming. Dim the lights, play soft music, and lay pillows around.
5. Before starting the ritual, think about what you want to achieve. Do you want to honor your ancestors, ask for guidance, say thank you, or all of the above? Having a purpose for your ritual will help you stay connected to it.
6. Cast a protection circle. (Go to chapter 5, exercise 2.)
7. Sit in the circle and take three deep breaths. Feel the ground beneath you and imagine roots anchoring your body into the earth.
8. Invite your ancestors' presence by lighting a candle or burning some incense. Choose a candle that feels right for the occasion, and as it burns, think of it as a beacon guiding your ancestors to you. If you're using incense, let the smoke rise and carry your prayers and intentions to the spirit world.
9. Now that your candle or incense is lit, invite your ancestors to join you. Speak to them. Say, "Dear ancestors, I welcome you into this sacred space. I honor your journeys and the wisdom you've shared with our family. Please come and be with me."
10. Say how grateful you are for them, their strength, and their guidance. You could say, "Thank you for your courage. I honor your sacrifices and the love you brought to our family. Your stories inspire me every day."

11. This part is optional, but you can place a small offering on the altar as a show of respect and connection. This offering could be a bowl of water to symbolize flow and ancestral wisdom. You can also bring flowers. Fresh flowers represent beauty and the cycle of life. Some people prefer to offer food since it is a more traditional offering during rituals.
12. When you place the offering on the altar, you can say, "With this gift, I honor you and the love that connects our family."
13. After thanking them and making your offering, sit with them in meditation. How does it feel to connect with your ancestors? Are you getting any thoughts or feelings at all? Sit silently for a few minutes and talk to them.
14. To conclude, thank your ancestors for being present with you and end the ritual with a positive affirmation. Say, "I honor my ancestors, their journeys, and the wisdom they have passed to me. May this connection bring healing and peace to our family."
15. Take some more deep breaths before you stand up and dismantle the protection circle.

Exercise 3: Visualization (Reclaiming Power from the Ancestors)

1. Sit or lie down in a comfortable position. Close your eyes and inhale deeply through your nose, exhaling slowly through your mouth.
2. Imagine your family tree as a giant, luminescent tree. The tree is full of life and energy, and it represents your lineage.
3. Hone in on the roots of the tree. Imagine them stretching deep into the earth, plunging far below the surface. These roots connect you to your ancestors as you draw on their strength and wisdom.
4. Shift your attention to the tree branches. See them reaching high into the sky, spreading out in all directions. Each branch represents a different branch of your family, your parents, grandparents, and so on. Picture the leaves shimmering in the sunlight, each one symbolizing the lives and stories of your ancestors.
5. Hold this image in your mind.

6. Now, invite any ancestor to join you, one at a time. Say their name.
7. Wait until you feel their presence. Imagine them standing beside you, looking at you with warmth and love. You might see their face clearly or only feel their energy, but you know for a fact that they are there. Trust that they are here to support you.
8. Now, imagine this ancestor offering you a symbol that represents their power. This could be anything – a glowing orb, jewelry, a feather or a flower.
9. Take this gift from them carefully and with intention. Accept it with gratitude. Feel its energy flow into you as you hold it. The gift is filling you with strength and inspiration. Thank your ancestor for their presence and the gift they have shared with you.
10. Feel the connection between you two and know that the bond is strong and will continue to support you all your life.
11. When you're ready, open your eyes and get your journal to write down everything you felt and heard during the visualization. These are messages from your ancestors. There might be answers to your current problems somewhere in those messages.

Chapter Eight: Creating a New Legacy: Spreading Healing Across Generations

The past is a book that has already been written. You can't go back and change the words on the pages, regardless of how much you wish you could. The past may still affect the present, but it's still the past. The healing work you do today is more for future generations than it is for the ancestors themselves. Of course, when you repair the bloodline, heal the wounds, and transmute the trauma, you are honoring and caring for your ancestors, but most of that work is for the present and the future.

Create a new legacy by healing across generations.[38]

You're doing more than preserving the past; you're investing in the future. You're making the home stronger, safer, and more livable for generations that will come after you. Think, for a second, how much easier their lives will be because you did the hard work, mending the broken pieces. They won't have to carry the same burdens you have. You're giving them a gift.

The life you live today will affect tomorrow's generations the same way the past has affected yours. Every time you choose to forgive, let go of resentment, or break a negative family pattern, you make a small deposit, similar to when you save for your child's college fund. You may only be able to put away a little bit each month, and it may not seem like a lot now, but one day, it'll be enough to send them to college. You, too, will be in the past one day. The question is, what kind of ancestor do you want to become?

Do you want to be the ancestor stuck in bitterness and resentment? Or do you want to be the one who broke the cycle and showed your family what it means to heal, grow, and create something better? It's not always easy to make the right choice. Forgiveness can be hard, and releasing resentment can feel like you're betraying yourself, but the decisions you make or don't make will influence the circumstances in which your children are born and raised. What kind of legacy do you want to leave behind?

Intentional Ancestry

This growing movement encourages people to be more intentional about their family histories and their legacies. It stresses that a family's history is not a random collection of names and figures but a narrative that influences the present and the future. Everyone is an important player in an ongoing story. It's a million stories inside a single story, and your story matters to the overarching plot.

A major goal of the intentional ancestry movement is to encourage people to actively research and document their family histories, not just to collect information but so they can better understand where they came from and how their ancestors' lives have engineered their lives. This might mean interviewing older family members, scouring historical records, or going as far as DNA testing to find previously unknown connections and branches of the family tree.

With a better grasp of their family histories, people are encouraged to think about the legacy they want to build before joining the ancestors. This involves distinguishing family values, traditions, and accomplishments that are most important to them and finding ways to preserve and pass them down to future generations. They're also encouraged to do what you're doing right now, which is pinpointing and confronting the difficult or painful narratives in their family history and using that knowledge to break damaging cycles, not only for their sake - but for their children and the children after them.

To live as an intentional potential ancestor, try this questionnaire:

- What are the earliest memories you have of your family traditions or rituals? What were the special things your family did together, like holidays, Sunday dinners, or bedtime routines? These early memories have clues about the values and identity that were important to your family - values you may want to carry forward.

- Are there any heirlooms, artifacts, or keepsakes that have special meaning in your family? Families typically have items that have been handed down, like jewelry, photo albums, or maybe furniture. You may want to preserve these for the next generation.

- Who are the elders in your family that you seek wisdom and guidance from? These older relatives, like your grandparents, aunts, and uncles, can teach so much to the younger generations.

- What values or principles did your parents or grandparents try to instill in you? You were raised based on the beliefs and ideals that were important to your family, so what lessons, morals, or character traits were emphasized in your childhood?

- Are there any family recipes, skills, or talents that have survived many generations? These need to be preserved as an honor to your heritage.

- Have you or any of your relatives ever attempted genealogical research to trace your family tree?

- Are there any family sayings or inside jokes?

- How have the geographical origins or migrations of your ancestors influenced your family's culture? The origin of your family and the journeys they've had to take over the centuries influenced everything from your values and traditions to your physical features and accents. The more you understand about them, the better.

- What are some of the proudest achievements or accomplishments in your family's history? Who started a business? Did someone serve in the military? Who was the first individual in the family to graduate from college?

- Are there any mental or physical health or addiction issues that have affected multiple generations? You can't do anything to prevent them from affecting future generations if you don't know they exist.

- How do the gender roles and family dynamics of previous eras show up in your family today?

- What are the most important lessons you've learned from the older members of your family?

- How do you hope to carry on or reinvent your family's traditions for future generations?

- What is the single most important thing you want your children or grandchildren to learn from your family's legacy?

At the end of the day, out of all the things you hope to do for your legacy, the very best one is to live authentically. Be true to yourself and let your personality and values shine brighter than the sun in all your actions. Your family traditions are important, but you should never be someone you're not. You can honor your ancestry and still blaze your own trail. Your genuine, unapologetic life will inspire future generations to do the same and might even inspire your family members right now. There are already too many masks and facades outside the family; there should be no need for them inside.

Your legacy will be defined not by accolades or achievements but by how you lived your life and if you lived with great qualities such as honesty, integrity, and compassion. That is the greatest gift you can leave behind.

Exercise 1: Write Your Legacy Letter

1. Go to a quiet place where you can think and reflect. Bring a notebook with you.
2. Breathe and prepare your mind.
3. In your mind's eye, imagine the people who will read your letter. They could be your children, grandchildren, or future generations. Think about what you want them to know about you and your life.
4. Decide on what you want to achieve with your letter. Do you want to share wisdom or stories? Do you want to tell them you love them?
5. After setting your intention, you can start writing. See if any of these prompts help:
    - Explain how your most problematic experiences changed you.
    - What advice would you give your younger self?
    - What negative behaviors did you notice in your family? How did you recognize them?
    - Were you able to help your family change those behaviors? How?
    - What family traditions do you love the most?
    - What values do you want your family to carry forward?
6. When you're finished with your letter, tear it out of the notebook, fold it, and put it in a safe, special place, maybe a family album or a keepsake box. Give it to your children one day if you'd like to have children – or to your nieces and nephews. As long as it makes it to the next generation, you succeeded!

Exercise 2: Legacy Vision Board

For this exercise, you'll be creating a vision board, not a traditional one for personal goals, but one that represents the values, traits, and traditions you wish to leave for future generations.

Create a legacy vision board."

To get started, you'll need a few simple materials:

- A large piece of cardboard, poster board, or corkboard
- Magazines, newspapers, printouts, or other inspirational pictures
- Scissors and glue or tape
- Markers or pens or both
- A journal

1. Before you start cutting and pasting, do some self-reflection. Ask yourself, "What's the legacy I want to leave?" "What mark do I want to have on the world?" "What do I want to be remembered for?"

2. Write down your first thoughts in your journal. You may want to be known for your kindness and compassion. Or you'd love to open a nonprofit that guarantees education to underserved communities. Or you simply want to raise children who act with integrity and service. Whatever your answer, let it be the truth. Be honest with yourself about the mark you want to make.

3. With your "why" in mind, start collecting images, words, and anything that's a symbol of your why. Flip through magazines, search the internet, or look through your own photos. Anything that captures the qualities, causes, or contributions you want to be known for, even if you're not sure exactly how it fits. Collecting these materials alone can be just as illuminating as the final vision board.

4. As soon as you have your materials together, you need to assemble your vision board.
5. Lay your background first. This could be a large poster that encapsulates the central idea or a patchwork of words, phrases, and smaller pictures. Let your intuition guide you as you play with the placement and composition.
6. Add the major materials that represent your legacy. This could be photos of role models who inspire you, pictures related to causes you care about, or personal mementos. Arrange these focal points intentionally so that they anchor the central design.
7. Fill in the gaps with supporting details like affirmations, sketches, fabric swatches, or anything aesthetically pleasing. These supplementary elements help flesh out the vision board and bring it to life.
8. Pause every once in a while and think. Does the board mirror the legacy you described in your journal? Does it feel cohesive and true to your values? Make all the adjustments you need until you're satisfied.
9. As time goes on, keep revisiting your vision board because there will be updates and additions as your vision evolves.

Exercise 3: Daily Legacy Practice

A daily legacy practice is a simple ritual that is built into your routine to help you radiate the values, qualities, and positive influence you want to leave behind. It pushes you to take small, intentional steps every day to take your legacy from dreams to reality.

1. Of course, the first step is to reflect on the legacy you hope to create. What are the qualities, behaviors, or contributions that are most important to you? These will be the basis for your daily practice. For example, suppose you want to be remembered as a compassionate person. In that case, you may need to perform one small act of kindness every day as your daily practice. What you choose is up to you as long as it is worthwhile and doable for you.
2. The next step is to make your legacy practice a consistent habit. Habits are powerful because they happen automatically without having to rely on willpower or motivation, and the best way to

build a habit is to link it to an existing routine. For example, performing your act of kindness on your way to work every day. It's a fact that attaching a new practice to an existing habit makes it much more likely to stick.

3. You can also try setting reminders or alerts on your phone or calendar to reinforce your new routine.
4. As you settle into your new practice, check in with yourself regularly. How is it going? Where do you need to make adjustments?
5. Track your progress in your journal so you don't miss patterns, and celebrate every milestone you achieve.
6. Establishing a new habit, *any habit*, is never easy, but keep showing up, even on the days when you'd rather not, and your habit will quickly become automatic.

Exercise 4: Intergenerational Rituals

Family rituals exist to connect family members with shared experiences and happy memories. There could already be traditions and rituals in your family, but there's no rule about adding another one. After all, a family ritual that lasts for ten generations could start with you.

The best family rituals are the ones everyone likes, so you can either do this by trial and error or you can go around asking for all of their input. You could start a gratitude ritual where, before dinner, everyone shares something they're grateful for. Or you could pick one night every month for storytelling – everyone gets a turn while everyone else has to listen to their story. The best part (or worst part, depending on your perspective) is that the storyteller gets to pick the story.

If family members move away or there are new additions to the family, include them. If something about the ritual is outdated, update it. Keep it fun and relevant. That way, the ritual grows and grows. Also, take pictures. Years later, you'll be grateful you did.

Exercise 5: Embodying the Future Self Meditation

1. Sit comfortably in a quiet room. Inhale deeply through your nose and exhale through your mouth.
2. Imagine yourself many years from now as the wise and loving ancestor you hope to become one day. What qualities define this future version of you? What does this future self look like? How do they carry themselves?
3. Imagine the warmth in their eyes and the kindness in their smile.
4. Move your attention to this future self's heart. What emotions do you feel from them? Do you feel unconditional love? Understanding? Strength? Feel their feelings within your own chest. Feel the love and wisdom they wish to pass down to their descendants.
5. With this image firmly in your mind, silently affirm your intention to manifest these qualities in yourself. Declare your commitment to living in alignment with the values and priorities that you want to be remembered for.
6. Now, bring your attention back to the present.
7. Take some more deep breaths.
8. Write everything you heard, saw, and felt in your journal. It'll be your motivation, a reminder of your promise to build a better legacy.

Conclusion

The work you have begun in your lineage is going to change your life and the lives of those around you forever. There is nothing easy about connecting to and attempting to heal the karma in your ancestry. It takes courage, vulnerability, and a commitment to face the parts of yourself and your family history that you may have preferred to keep buried. It is one of the greatest gifts anyone can possibly give, and there you are, doing it. You're doing it scared. You're doing it tired. You're doing it with grace.

There may have been moments when you've wanted to give up, ignore all of it and go back to your comfortable, familiar habits. It would be so much easier, wouldn't it? To pretend those shadows don't exist and continue living your life the way you always have, but something deep inside you knows that avoidance is far too expensive. You've glimpsed the freedom, the peace, the possibility that lies on the other side of this healing work, and now that you've seen it, there's no going back. Your soul and ancestors are calling you forward, even when your mind and body want nothing more than to take off your armor.

So, you show up again and again. You keep doing the meditations, the rituals, the difficult conversations with your family. You keep shedding generations' worth of conditioning, toxic beliefs, and destructive patterns. It's grueling, emotional work, but you know, in your very depths, that it's necessary.

There's no rulebook or timeline for how it's "supposed" to unfold. Your healing journey is your own and no one else's. Honor that and give yourself permission to move at your own pace. Thousands of others around the world are on this healing path. They're reconnecting with their roots and detangling the intergenerational traumas that have kept their bloodline bound for too long. You are part of a growing movement, a collective transformation that is sweeping across the planet.

Your ancestors are walking alongside you every step of the way. They see your courage, they feel your vulnerability, and they are grateful for the work you are doing. Whenever you feel uncertain or discouraged, call them. Invite them to guide you, to lend you their strength, and to light the way in the dark. You are doing inner work that is so desperately needed for yourself and for all the generations ahead of you. Keep going. Keep showing up. This is your legacy. This is your gift to the world.

If you enjoyed this book, I'd greatly appreciate a review on Amazon because it helps me to create more books that people want. It would mean a lot to hear from you.

To leave a review:
1. Open your camera app.
2. Point your mobile device at the QR code.
3. The review page will appear in your web browser.

Thanks for your support!

Here's another book by Mari Silva that you might like

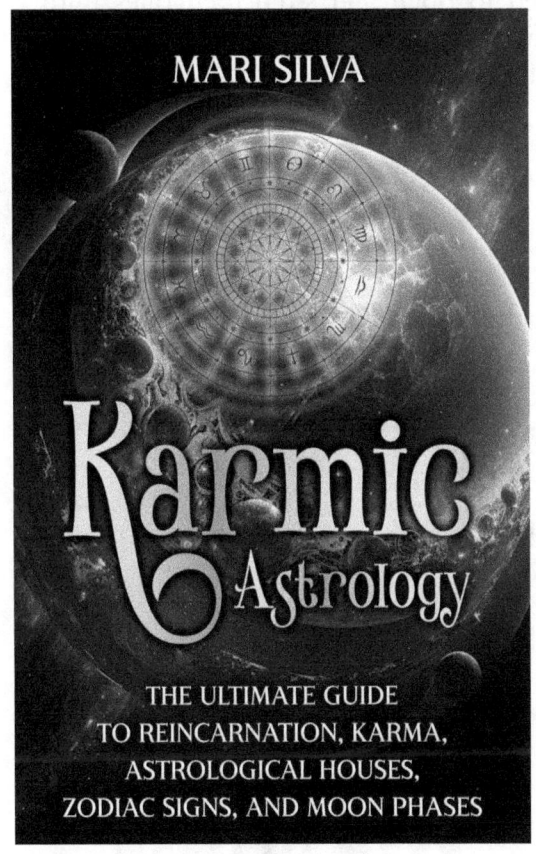

Your Free Gift
(only available for a limited time)

Thanks for getting this book! If you want to learn more about various spirituality topics, then join Mari Silva's community and get a free guided meditation MP3 for awakening your third eye. This guided meditation mp3 is designed to open and strengthen ones third eye so you can experience a higher state of consciousness. Simply visit the link below the image to get started.

https://spiritualityspot.com/meditation
Or, Scan the QR code!

References

Brandon. (2024, December 12). *What is Ho'oponopono? | Original Prayer, Effects & History.* WE FREE SPIRITS. https://wefreespirits.com/hooponopono-prayer-effects-history/

Brooklyn Somatic Therapy. (2025, February 18). Brooklyn Somatic Therapy. https://www.brooklynsomatictherapy.com/blog/understanding-family-constellations-a-path-to-deep-healing

Farmer, S. (2014). *Healing Ancestral Karma.* Hierophant Publishing.

Jackson, L. (2022, March 29). *Carl Jung and the Shadow: Everything you need to know.* Hack Spirit. https://hackspirit.com/carl-jung-and-the-shadow/

Jampolsky, G. G. (2011). *Forgiveness.* Simon and Schuster.

Kaufman, J., Khan, M., Shepard Payne, J., Mancini, J., & Summers White, Y. (2023). Transgenerational Inheritance and Systemic Racism in America. *Psychiatric Research and Clinical Practice, 5*(2), n/a-n/a. https://doi.org/10.1176/appi.prcp.20220043

teaandrosemary2. (2022, November 20). *How To Cast A Circle: The Ultimate Guide For Practitioners.* Tea & Rosemary. https://teaandrosemary.com/how-to-cast-a-circle/

Wein, H. (2010, September 27). *Stress hormone causes epigenetic changes.* National Institutes of Health (NIH). https://www.nih.gov/news-events/nih-research-matters/stress-hormone-causes-epigenetic-changes

What is Ancestral Healing? - Sacred Ancestry. (2020, May 23). *Sacred Ancestry.* Sacred Ancestry. https://www.sacredancestry.com/blog/what-is-ancestral-healing-blog

Wohl, N. (2024, December 31). *Tona Therapy, LCSW, PLLC.* Tona Therapy, LCSW, PLLC. https://www.tonatherapy.com/blog/how-trauma-lives-in-your-body

Image Sources

1 Photo by Mikhail Nilov: https://www.pexels.com/photo/person-holding-lighted-candles-7705395/

2 Image by Agata from Pixabay https://pixabay.com/vectors/family-tree-genealogical-tree-6095395/

3 Kenny Louie from Vancouver, Canada, CC BY 2.0 <https://creativecommons.org/licenses/by/2.0>, via Wikimedia Commons https://commons.wikimedia.org/wiki/File:Chaos_Theory_(2943904661).jpg

4 Photo by Nicola Barts : https://www.pexels.com/photo/man-holding-a-leather-wallet-7927426/

5 Photo by Kalz 📷 UG Michael: https://www.pexels.com/photo/selective-focus-grayscale-photo-of-women-in-face-paint-lying-down-posing-with-her-finger-on-her-lips-2486421/

6 Photo by Amsterdam City Archives on Unsplash https://unsplash.com/photos/z_at8cVoINU

7 Images are generated by Life Science Databases(LSDB)., CC BY-SA 2.1 JP <https://creativecommons.org/licenses/by-sa/2.1/jp/deed.en>, via Wikimedia Commons https://commons.wikimedia.org/wiki/File:Hippocampus_image.png

8 http://www.memorylossonline.com/glossary/amygdala.html, CC0, via Wikimedia Commons https://commons.wikimedia.org/wiki/File:Amygdala.jpg

9 Photo by Mumtahina Tanni: https://www.pexels.com/photo/shadow-of-a-person-standing-on-stairs-6472771/

10 Photo by cottonbro studio: https://www.pexels.com/photo/a-boy-watching-her-parents-quarrel-6603348/

11 Photo by Josh Hild: https://www.pexels.com/photo/photo-of-empty-road-in-between-grass-field-during-golden-hour-2801312/

12 Photo by Tim Grundtner: https://www.pexels.com/photo/woman-in-white-dress-falling-on-gray-concrete-floor-3856635/

13 Photo by RF._.studio _: https://www.pexels.com/photo/woman-in-black-tank-top-and-black-pants-sitting-on-concrete-floor-3820312/

14 jsjgeology, Attribution 2.0 Generic, CC BY 2.0 <https://creativecommons.org/licenses/by/2.0/deed.en> https://www.flickr.com/photos/jsjgeology/48680181172

15 Marie-Lan Taÿ Pamart, CC BY 4.0 <https://creativecommons.org/licenses/by/4.0>, via Wikimedia Commons https://commons.wikimedia.org/wiki/File:Amethyst_Siberia_MNHN_Min%C3%A9ralogie.jpg

16 Cedaric, CC BY-SA 2.0 <https://creativecommons.org/licenses/by-sa/2.0>, via Wikimedia Commons https://commons.wikimedia.org/wiki/File:Citrine_(10902015484).jpg

17 / rockandmineralplanet.com, Attribution-ShareAlike 4.0 International, CC BY-SA 4.0 <https://creativecommons.org/licenses/by-sa/4.0/deed.en> via Wikimedia Commons https://commons.wikimedia.org/wiki/File:Carnelian_flame.jpg

18 Photo by Quang Nguyen Vinh: https://www.pexels.com/photo/women-holding-sky-lantern-against-blue-sky-6872503/

19 https://www.flickr.com/photos/volvob12b/10721985945

20 Photo by Markus Spiske: https://www.pexels.com/photo/grey-chain-link-on-brown-concrete-floor-260032/

21 Photo by Ketut Subiyanto: https://www.pexels.com/photo/crop-unrecognizable-black-man-writing-in-notebook-on-balcony-4559968/

22 Photo by Pavel Danilyuk: https://www.pexels.com/photo/grayscale-photography-of-a-person-sitting-beside-the-table-with-picture-frame-8057075/

23 Photo by RDNE Stock project: https://www.pexels.com/photo/women-sitting-on-the-couch-7951553/

24 Photo by Mikhail Nilov: https://www.pexels.com/photo/woman-pinning-photos-on-corkboard-6932086/